DAILY INFUSIONS OF HOPE

The Narrow Road

DR. MICHELE SHERWOOD
DR. MARK SHERWOOD

www.Sherwood.TV

The Narrow Road
Daily Infusions of Hope

Dr. Michele Sherwood and Dr. Mark Sherwood
© 2023 Hope Dealers International

All rights reserved. Except as permitted under the U.S. Copyright Act of 1976, no part of this publication may be reproduced, distributed, or transmitted in any form or by any means, or stored in a database or retrieval system, without the prior written permission of the publisher.

Unless otherwise noted, scripture taken from the Holy Bible, NEW INTERNATIONAL VERSION®, NIV® Copyright © 1973, 1978, 1984, 2011 by Biblica, Inc.® Used by permission. All rights reserved worldwide.

Printed in the United States of America

A note to the reader:

This book is not intended as a substitute for the medical advice of physicians. The reader should regularly consult a physician in matters relating to their health and particularly with respect to any symptoms that may require diagnosis or medical attention.

www.Sherwood.tv
www.FMIDR.com

―――――――

This book is dedicated to the legacy of my (Dr Michele's) mom, Sara M. Gosen-Neil. Through all her physical struggles, she never stepped away from her faith! She was the inspiration for my tapestry with a pen, and my grit to never quit.

Also, to my (Dr Michele's) grandfather Rev. Kenneth L. Roufs, a man who committed his life to spreading hope to his dear ones. He asked me to carry on his work of spreading hope, health, and healing to the world.

Finally, we honor our wonderful patients and supporters around the world who inspire us every day.

―――――――

INTRODUCTION
A Daily Walk On The Narrow Road

"Enter through the narrow gate. For wide is the gate and broad is the road that leads to destruction, and many enter through it. But small is the gate and narrow the road that leads to life, and only a few find it."
(MATTHEW 7:13-14)

Thank you for walking through these readings with us!

We wrote them for you, but they're also an expression of our daily steps and struggles as we follow God.

Rather than a book full of teachings, you'll discover that we're simply sharing our thoughts and challenges as they came to us. And the only way to stay on this narrow road, is by the grace of God and the power in His Word.

There's no pressure to read a devotional every day. That's why there's not 365 of them. Go at your own pace. Read two one day or stay with one reading for three days. If the words are speaking life to you in a special way, keep meditating on that reading as long as you need.

We've also included, in the paperback version, space for writing your impressions and prayers. Taking time to pause and reflect on God's Word is essential. Write your thoughts and questions, and copy the scriptures that minister life to you. Writing and speaking the Word is another way to bring peace and renew your mind.

You'll see that we cover many topics and themes, including spiritual health, mental health, and physical health. But all these readings are centered on following God closely (even if imperfectly) on the narrow path that leads to Life.

We believe in you!

1
Right side up in and upside-down world

DR. MICHELE

Last night was a great time at the Night of Empowerment, our quarterly community event. We love to minister to people and enjoy seeing lives changed. Last night's theme was "Living right side up in and upside-down world."

Two keys are important to pursue this.

First, we have to resolve to be courageous. Courage does not come at the time of testing. Courage is formed by previous tests. Courage does not simply appear. It is forged in the trials of temptation to quit. Quitting is easy. Staying the course in the trials and tribulations builds courage. It builds diamonds from the rough.

Second, in trying times, and at all times, we must speak with a boldness and confidence when we stand witness to lies and issues that obviously need change. We must rely on a God that is bigger than us.

Alone we are nothing. In him we are everything we need to be. This is not ego or pride, it is a dependance on our Father in heaven who knows our hearts and wants us to lean on Him.

> "Does anyone want to live a life that is long and prosperous? Then keep your tongue from speaking evil and your lips from telling lies. Turn away from evil and do good. Search for peace, and work to maintain it. (Psalm 34:12-14, NLT)

In todays world it seems what was wrong is now right, what was illegal is now legal, what was unethical is now ethical. People who live by Biblical standards are considered radical and people who question what doesn't seem right are demonized.

All of this confusion can make one weary. Again we find peace in scripture.

> "I have told you these things, so that in me you may have peace. In this world you may have trouble. But take heart! I have overcome the world." (JOHN 16:33)

These scriptures encourage us and bring promise. Be courageous in this world of trouble. Speak with a boldness and confidence in all areas that need correction. This is when favor from the Lord is granted. We see wisdom in action displayed. The world will see you differently. You will hear more from God above and uncommon promotion will follow. This does not always mean a money or job promotion. You will see doors open and blessings flow. It takes being obedient in all ways.

Mark and I aim to live courageously and speak with boldness. We also take a stand to stay on the narrow path. The wide road is easy and lacks courage. Our prayer is that you see us being courageous, speaking with boldness, and witnessing more of Jesus working through our lives to bless yours. And we pray to see this in you.

Live the "wellness" life with us, right-side up. We believe in you.

_____

_____

_____

_____

_____

_____

2
You Are Protected

DR. MICHELE

EVER FEEL LIKE YOU ARE ON FIRE AND BEING SCORCHED? EVER FEEL like you are about to drown?

The truth is, you are protected.

> *"When you pass through the waters, I will be with you, and through the rivers, they will not overwhelm you. When you walk through the fire, you will not be burned or scorched, nor will the flame kindle upon you."* (ISAIAH 43:2)

As with the children of Israel, God will part the sea, so we can walk through. We may be in the storm but the storm is not in us. Jesus is with us in the storm.

Like the three Hebrew boys in the fiery furnace, Jesus is with us. God does not fail or falter at His promise. "Hold thou me up, and I shall be safe: and I will have respect unto thy statutes continually." (PSALM 119:117)

"Show me your glory, God," Moses begged.

We cross a line when we make such a request. When our deepest desire is not the blessings of God, or a favor from God, but God Himself, we cross a threshold. Less self-focus, more God-focus. Less about me, more about Him.

We all are challenged every day to see the bigger picture. Only when we abide in God, will we see His life and love, and see how we fit into His plans.

3
It's Not Tricky or Mysterious

DR. MARK

WHAT IS GOD'S INTENT REGARDING OUR HEALTH?

This question is not a trick or a mystery. The answer should be obvious. It's intended to make one think, *Does God really want us to walk in health?* Let's examine the Word of God in regard to this question.

> "And these signs will follow those who believe: in My name they will cast out demons; they will speak with new tongues; they will take up servants; and if they drink anything deadly, it will by no means hurt them; they will lay hands on the sick, and they will recover."
> (MARK 16:17-18 NKJV)

Notice the last concept of laying hands on the sick. Does it say they *might* recover? And does it say, their disease will be *managed*? Quite the contrary. This is a positive, affirmative, and sure statement. They will recover. So let's say this in a different way, in terms we understand: the sick will be healed and not simply be managed.

Let's examine one more scripture:

> "Beloved, I pray that you may prosper in all things and be in health, just as your soul prospers." (3 JOHN 2 NKJV)

It should become obvious at this point that walking in health is indeed God's intention for his children. Further, it is also His intent that his children (disciples) play an active role in bringing health to the world through the healing power of the Holy Spirit within us.

With that being established, it is very curious that the following statistics exist in the United States:

Heart disease is still the number one killer and has been for the last 40 years. Cancer is still killing the same number of persons per 100,000 as it was 40 years ago. Every 40 seconds someone has a heart attack. 2200 person die each day in the US of heart disease, and at least 250,000 people die of this disease process every year before reaching the hospital. Though the statistics are US-based, these disturbing trends are ongoing worldwide, indicating the western lifestyle, as we know it, is riddled with disease prediction.

Our world and the next generation is being affected severely. We are losing a generation and MUST understand why that is, so that we can quickly do something about it.

Perhaps, we have been deceived into believing that simply managing a disease is the best God has for us.

Let's align our thoughts, words, and beliefs with the truth of God's word. You are His *dear one*, after all.

4
Where does Peace Come From?

DR. MICHELE

Sometimes Life seems full of roadblocks of one kind or another. Frustrating as that is, added frustration comes knowing we can't do anything about it.

Trying to crash through roadblocks only wastes energy and builds on the frustration already present. The "serenity prayer" adds some wisdom to solving the problem:

"God grant me the serenity to accept the things I cannot change."

And this scripture resets our perspective:

"The peace of God which surpasses all understanding will keep your hearts and minds in Christ Jesus." (Phil. 4:7)

Where does this peace come from? Another Scripture reveals its Source :

"Peace I leave with you, My peace I give to you. I do not give to you as the world gives. Let not our hearts be troubled, and do not let them be afraid." (John 14:27)

Jesus' peace, when allowed to permeate the heart, takes the "fever" out of those frustrations caused by our inability to make changes. His peace comes as a part of His free gift of grace made possible through His redeeming work. His gift of forgiveness and eternal life are free with no strings attached. Remember the hymn?

"When peace like a river attendeth my way, when sorrows like sea billows roll,
Whatever my lot, Thou hast taught me to say, 'It is well, it is well with my soul.'"

These words came from a man who couldn't change the fact that his beloved family had tragically perished. Only the Lord could give him such a gift of grace.

Mark and I haven't been able to solve some frustrating life issues. However we keep trusting and learning, believing that God is working it all for good.

We thank God that as we allow God's peace to do its work in us, a holy quietness floods our hearts. His peace takes over! Praise God, He didn't leave us in frustration, or peace-less!

5
A Refining Fire

DR. MICHELE

Sometimes life feels like a fiery furnace. It burns you, hurts you and leaves those unwanted and haunting soul wounds. When we look at scripture, it is healing and holds promise for the days ahead.

I reflect on Isaiah 48:10: "Behold, I have refined you, but not as silver. I have tested you in the furnace of affliction."

Through it all, we can rise to the occasion and dust the ashes off of our feet and move forward. Our Father in heaven is a righteous father and he protects us at all cost.

He does however lend us free will to chose. Often times those choices get us into the hands of trouble. It is easy to make bad choices. The devil will try to take you out. If he can't take you out, he will try and wear you out. Don't you dare get tired. Hold on because our Father is always there.

Scripture tells us in Jeremiah 17:7: "But I will bless the person who puts trust in me."

That is a simple promise. Put your trust in the Lord and do the right thing, in all things all the time. The blessings will follow and out of trouble, we will stay.

This is the work of our lives. Mark and I will honor our Father in heaven from whom all blessings flow. We know you want this, too. This is our prayer for your life and the lives of all those you love.

6
Where we place our trust

DR. MARK

WHY ARE SO MANY, SO SICK?

Hopefully, you have asked yourself, as we have asked ourselves many times, *Does God simply manage disease rather than heal?* And further, *Do we ever think there is a difference between healing disease and management of disease?*

Let us realize that God, in his awesomeness, is about total restoration. When Jesus walked the earth, instantaneous and amazing miracles occurred. The lame walked, the leprous were cleansed, the deaf heard, the blind saw, and the mute spoke. Imagine being a person living in that time in history. Wow, what incredible awe and wonder they must have experienced!

As Jesus affirmed in Mark 2:17: "Those who are well have no need for a physician, but those who are sick. I did not come to call the righteous, but sinners, to repentance."

Jesus clearly infers there are some who may not have known they were sick. But who are those people? Does it even seem possible that someone would be sick and not know it?

If Jesus came, died, rose again, and further deposited the Holy Spirit within us, why are so many people so sick? Has He failed us? Is His healing not applicable today? Quite the contrary, his Word, love, and power is just as strong in us, as believers, as it was when Jesus walked the earth. Yes, we have that same Holy Spirit in us that empowered Jesus to do the miracles He did.

Perhaps, a bit of deception or unbelief, has began to creep into our lives. Or, maybe we have believed that there is always "a pill to cure our ill" and that it was designed by God? Maybe there are some of us who are sick, don't realize it, and even been led to believe "sick" is normal?

There is little doubt that we see a huge upward trend in the usage of pharmaceutical drugs. The trend is disturbing in the sense that drugs are not designed to heal disease, but rather to manage disease conditions. If we believe that God's intent is to heal, we should pause and think. Let's examine the following scripture:

> "Now the works of the flesh are evident, which are: adultery, fornication, uncleanliness, lewdness, idolatry, sorcery, hatred, contentions, jealousies, outburst of wrath, selfish ambitions, dissensions..." (GALATIANS 5:19-20 NKJV)

Let's look at the word "sorcery." Translated in the original Greek, this word denotes the connotation of *pharmakeia*. Yes, that's correct. This is where the word *pharmacy* comes from. It literally means using drugs. I'm not saying medicine is bad; rather we are saying the dependence upon them to bring about healing is a falsehood. Additionally, the unnecessary and overuse of them is extremely dangerous and deadly.

Is there a better way? Yes, most definitely. There is something called *lifestyle*, which includes stress management, nutritional intake, sleep maximization, spiritual growth, financial management, relational health, God-directed medical guidance and instruction, and exercise. If these area all are addressed, we potentially see major reduction in the following, very common, disease processes: heart disease, type 2 diabetes, autoimmune conditions, osteoporosis, Alzheimer's disease, early onset dementia, and cancer.

It is estimated that 85%, or more, of these diseases are driven by mismanagement of lifestyle. Can you imagine cutting these diseases at that rate? Is God's intent of health partially tied to our willingness to *walk* in health? Notice these current chronically high disease conditions are dissimilar in nature of those Jesus came across while he walked the earth.

We must consider realigning our principles, teaching, and culture around improving overall lifestyle, and also consider reestablishing our belief system around God's original intent, rather than man's created design.

Let's place our trust in The Savior and true Healer.

7
Tried and Tested

DR. MICHELE

Each day we can be tried, tested, and tossed, and sometimes find ourselves unsteady. But hold on to this scripture from Isaiah 48.

> "Behold, I have refined you, but not as silver; I have tried and chosen you in the furnace of affliction."

Refining is a process where everything that is unwanted is removed. It brings pure gold out of the dirt.

At the time of testing it might appear as if God has left us, as the process is painful. Scripture reminds us that he will never leave us or forsake us! Don't let feelings lead you away from the truth.

He will refine us until He sees a reflection of Himself in us.

Just as parents correct and discipline a child they love dearly, so does our Heavenly Father. We are loved.

> "We went through fire and through water: but thou broughtest us out into a wealthy place."

> "But the Lord hath taken you, and brought you forth out of the iron furnace, even out of Egypt, to be unto him a people of inheritance, as ye are this day."

> "Hardships can be so painful, and our Father certainly encourages us to speak of those hardships to him. But opportunity says that hardships, for God's children, never come without hope. And, with practice, we can

discover that hope carries the most weight. Since God is sovereign and has good purposes, hardships are opportunities." (Edward T. Welch)

Today, choose to draw closer to God, even in the trials. He is bringing out the best in us!

8
Righteous Anger

DR. MICHELE

Remember the occasion at the temple, when Jesus became angry? Took a whip! Really, He seemed quite "ticked-off" about the misuse of a holy place by some. Instead of using it as a place of worship, they made it a place to "make a buck."

We call Jesus' response, "Righteous anger."

Yes, there seemed to be times when the Lord showed his displeasure expressed in anger; especially, when he sees his children living in such defiant disobedience.

From Psalm 3:5, we read:

"His anger is for a moment, but His favor is for a lifetime. Weeping may endure for a night, but joy comes with the morning."

Thus, we may not understand why something we don't want messes up our lives and we may even think that the Lord is really angry with us. However, our thoughts ought not to be focused on our perceived God's short-lived anger, but on His long-term mercy which lasts for a lifetime.

His love works that way! That's what brings the joy of a new day. We have the opportunity to live right, do right, and be right in all ways. The choice is up to us.

That is our hope for our lives too. Mark and I will stand corrected if our lives displease the Lord and know that joy comes in the morning with the dawn of a new day.

Draw near to God with an open heart, right now. Receive His correction, and mercy. Enjoy His favor and guidance.

9
Dirt Suits?

DR. MARK

Are we expecting a pill to cure our ill? Is this really the best God can do? Certainly not. So what really happened to get us off course?

Let's go back to the beginning and try to establish a clear picture of what God's kingdom and his healing principles are truly are.

In Genesis 1:26, God said, "Let us make man in our image, according to our likeness; let them have dominion over the fish in the sea, the birds of the air, over the cattle, over all the earth and over every living thing that creeps on the earth."

The key point of the scripture is that God gave us dominion. That was dominion over all these animals and birds, as well as the earth. Dominion means to prevail, reign, rule over, or dominate. Let's keep that in mind as we move forward.

Genesis 1:29 reads, "see, I have given you every herb that yields seed which is on the face of the earth, and every tree fruit yields seed; to you it shall be given for food."

It is interesting to note that God gave dominion to man over the same earth which yields food for man's existence. Please note that God actually gave appetite for plants when he created us.

The unhealthy appetite that we may battle (whether to have non-nutrient anti-foods which yield disease *or* God-created life-giving foods which yield health) is really a choice between giving complete control to God or succumbing to self, which is our greatest destructive force.

Let's look at one more scripture to really drive this point home.

Genesis 2:7: "and the Lord formed man out of the dust of the crowd, and breathed into his nostrils the breath of life; and man became a living being."

Said another way, God made man out of the same ground in which He gave him dominion over. Therefore, God gives us dominion over the body which was created by dirt. That's right. You and I are running around every day in our *dirt suit*.

Are we truly caring for this miraculous creation that was handcrafted by our heavenly father? Or are we giving over control to poor choices.

Genesis 2:9: "and out of the ground the Lord God made every tree grow that is pleasant to the site and good for food."

Have you ever heard a child say, "I hate vegetables?" Have you ever said it? I know I have. When I was a child, I said that phrase so many times I care not to remember. How inaccurate and deceiving it is when you think about it! If God made all these nutrient-containing beautiful plants, including vegetables, for our good, why would we ever express hatred.

Now that we have established the concept of dominion and God creating appetite, as well as food, through plants, for the body, here are some not so funny certainties about God's creation.

There were no chicken nugget trees, doughnut bushes, and french fry shrubs in the garden of Eden. The was not a cola river or milkshake lake.

Then why do we even allow them to be served to anyone we love, including ourselves?

Take good care of your dirt suit today, okay? Healthy habits happen one day at a time.

10
Clean Power

DR. MICHELE

We are doing a two-week detox as a group in the clinic. But we're not only detoxing from food, we're detoxing from unhealthy emotions.

It's always amazing to me to come face-to-face with emotional health that I think has been cleared away from the barracks of my mind and heart long ago. Emotions are fickle, they're still around. So grateful we have our Lord and Savior to lean on. The wounds of the past can leave one bitter, unsettled, and tense in everyday life. Disappointments add up and grab hold of the heart, and twist emotional health. That's not a fun way to live.

Galatians 5:22-23 reminds us of the fruits of the Spirit. It's always refreshing to put on the right clothing we should wear every day.

> "But the fruit of the Spirit is love, joy, peace, long-suffering, kindness, goodness, faithfulness, gentleness, self-control. Against such there is no law."

During this detox I found myself once again having to revisit forgiveness! Forgiveness frees us up!

"If we confess our sins, He is faithful and just to forgive us our sins and to cleanse us from all unrighteousness."

Wow, what a cleansing! We are forgiven. And we must forgive ourselves and others equally in order to have complete freedom. I'll take that detox!

When renewing my mind daily, and even hourly, a few verses from come to mind:

> "God grant you to be strengthened in your inner being with the power of His Spirit and that Christ may dwell in your hearts through faith, as

you are being rooted and grounded in love. I pray that you may have the power to comprehend with all the saints, what is the breadth, and length, and height, and depth, and to know the love of Christ which surpasses knowledge so that you may be filled with all the fullness of God. Now to Him who by the power at work within us is able to accomplish abundantly far more than all we can ask or imagine." (Col. 3:17-20)

Let's take a deep breath and accept the fact that good and bad emotions and thoughts exist within each of us. Which power do we really want to be at work in our lives? We can choose to destroy ourselves with unhealthy habits or build ourselves with right use of action and right thinking.

Checking "past records" we must admit that too often we "plug in" to the evil, or, bad powers. That's when we do what messes up our lives. Thus, the time comes to "unplug" that power source!

The above verses encourage us to be connected with the Spirit's power. Jesus came to make that "plug in" available to all of us. Power to live right with our God and people around us, power to be morally and spiritually strong, power to love genuinely, power to overcome temptations and bad habits, power to believe in Jesus even during those difficult events that do happen.

Note: line from above verses: "that Christ may dwell in your hearts through faith." See? Faith in Jesus "plugs us in" to God's wonder-working power!

Plug in right now and be filled.

11
The Goodness and Sovereignty of God

DR. MICHELE

I AM GRATEFUL FOR HONEST PEOPLE. I AM GRATEFUL FOR PEOPLE THAT keep their word. I am grateful for people who think about others instead of only " ME, ME, ME." Focus on self is part of our fallen American values. It appears that the majority think only about themselves when the going gets tough.

People break their promises, they violate their written contracts, all in the name of self. These are painful situations. They abandon not only their teammates, they abandon their friends and people who have been by their side in difficult times.

As a physician and one who signed an oath to help the sick and hurting, wouldn't it be just dandy when I get that call on a Saturday night from a person who has been hurt in an accident, broken an arm, and I answer, "-Sorry, I have to do what is right for me. I will see you later." Instead, I do what I can to help and find the best surgeon to save an arm.

How about the person involved in a toxic relationship, not just once but twice, someone in need of an ear and soulful help in times where jail terms are involved, where serious life-threatening issues are at stake?

In these tough times, I will not change my character or my commitment to being loyal and giving. The ones who value only themselves will have to deal with the pain they cause others. The story of Judas and his betrayal of Jesus still rings true.

The Bible clearly indicates that Judas was not saved. Jesus Himself said of Judas, "The Son of Man will go just as it is written about him. But woe to that man who betrays the Son of Man! It would be better for him if he had not been born." (MATTHEW 26:24). Here is a clear picture of the sovereignty of God and the will of man working together. God had, from ages past, determined that Christ would be betrayed by Judas, die on the cross for our sins, and be resurrected. Noting would stop the plan of God to provide salvation for mankind.

However, the fact that it was all foreordained does not excuse Judas or absolve him from the punishment he would suffer for his part in the drama. Judas made his own choices, and they were the source of his own damnation. Yet the choices fit perfectly into the sovereign plan of God. God controls not only the good, but also the evil of man to accomplish His own ends.

Here we see Jesus condemning Judas, but considering that Judas traveled with Jesus for nearly three years, we know He also gave Judas ample opportunity for salvation and repentance. Even after his dreadful deed, Judas could have fallen on his knees to beg God's forgiveness. But he did not. He may have felt some remorse born of fear, which caused him to return the money to the Pharisees, but he never repented, preferring instead to commit suicide. (MATTHEW 27:5-8)

In John 17:12, Jesus prays concerning His disciples, "While I was with them, I protected them and kept them safe by that name you gave me. None has been lost except the one doomed to destruction so that Scripture would be fulfilled." Jesus sent the disciples out to proclaim the gospel and perform miracles (LUKE 9:1-6). Judas was included in this group. Judas had faith, but it was not a true saving faith. Judas was never "saved," but for a time he was a follower of Christ.

We can be examples and love people intensely. We cannot control the ways of their hearts. Lessons learned. They are painful lessons. Yet taking an oath to always lend a hand, honor people, and continue to offer hope and healing for this hurting world is something we all must do.

No matter how someone has turned their back, stabbed the hearts of people, including their teammates, we will keep serving the Lord. Day and night, we will continue to uphold righteousness and model this example, by the grace God gives us.

We hope this will be your choice also.

12
Food for Thought

DR. MARK

Why are the choices seemingly so difficult?

Let's dive into some reasons why there seems to be such difficulty in making the right choices. The first reason stems from how we use our words.

Consider the common statement, "I hate vegetables." Certainly, this is not of God nor is it mimicking His character… especially knowing that he made those vegetables a necessity for our very existence and healing while we walk this earth.

Remember, our words are a creative force. They initiate a neuro-chemical storm within our neurological system that stimulates a variety of bodily actions. In other words, they unleash our bodies internal regulators to deal with life as we perceive it. If we so much as utter a phrase that declares we're "scared," we will be on some level. If we speak a phrase of "hate," we likely will. You get the idea.

Here are some scriptures to keep in mind:

Proverbs 11:9: "Evil words destroy one's friends; wise discernment rescues the godly."

Proverbs 11:2: "It is foolish to belittle a neighbor: a person with good sense remains silent."

Proverbs 11:17: "Your own soul is nourished when you are kind, but you destroy yourself when you are cruel."

Proverbs 15:1: "A gentle answer turns away wrath, but hard words stir up anger."

Proverbs 15:4: "Gentle words bring life and health; a deceitful tongue crushes the spirit."

Proverbs 16:24: "Kind words are like honey, sweet to the soul and healthy for the body."

Proverbs 18:4: "A person's words can be life-giving water; words of true wisdom are as refreshing as a bubbling brook."

Proverbs 18:20: "Words satisfy the soul as food satisfies the stomach; the right words on a person's lips bring satisfaction."

Our words do matter. These are just a few of many biblical statements concerning how we speak.

Perhaps we need to start proclaiming that we "love vegetables." Now that is certainly "food for thought."

I once challenged a pastor friend of mine, who incessantly stated he would never like vegetables, with a six month test. In the six months, he was to profess daily, "I *love* vegetables." He reluctantly agreed.

I would occasionally encourage him and remind him of our agreement. In the first couple of months, I could tell he wasn't liking this one bit. However, at the end of six months something miraculous happened. You guessed it. He was eating vegetables with every meal and actually loving them. His health improved and he lost a good amount of weight on top of that. He became a beacon of health and hope for many. Yes, he was actually speaking God's will, purpose, and intent over his life.

Maybe this is a challenge you'd consider. Do your words need to change regarding food and appetite?

_____

_____

_____

_____

_____

_____

_____

_____

13
Thinking and Thanking

DR. MICHELE

ONE DOESN'T HAVE TO LIVE LONG ON OUR PLANET BEFORE REALIZING that the components which make up life for us bring joy to the heart. Think of the multi-shaped, colored, and sweet-smelling flowers that beautify the landscape, which seasonally blossom, and can even grace our homes at special times of celebration.

Our Creator did that (many other things, too) for our happiness! How wonderful of the Lord to create this planet with our joy in mind! Then, Jesus comes along and He talks about bringing us joy: "I have said these things to you so that My joy may be in you and that your joy may be complete." (JOHN 15:11)

Yes, a different kind of joy, this is joy of the soul that comes from a life with meaning, purpose, peace of mind, a living hope, an assurance of sins forgiven, a right relationship in the royal family of our Creator and Redeemer, and so much more. What joys Jesus provides! But let's also remember what this provision cost Him.

On our reflective journey today, let us make time to ponder these mighty acts of God for the express purpose of our experiencing true joy, daily, no matter what happens.

Thinking such thoughts adds up to *thanking* the One who provides the most and the best, at great cost to Him. My, how He treasures us! We must be worth much in His eyes.

Ponder these truths, and share this message to remind others to look for the joy!

14
Life to the Full

DR. MICHELE

THIS IS THE DAY THAT THE LORD HAS MADE. LET US REJOICE AND BE glad in it. (PSALM 118:24)

The world can be a disturbing place. However, when we read the Bible (basic instructions before leaving earth) we know that darkness has a mission. Yet through our Lord, we can have an abundant life.

Scripture tells us in John 10:10, "The thief comes only to steal and kill and destroy; I have come that they may have life and have it to the full."

God is with us always, and with Him, darkness will flee. Let your heart and mind be at peace as you read this next scripture:

"And God is able to bless you abundantly, so that in all things at all times, having all that you need, you will abound in every good work".
(2 CORINTHIANS 9:8)

Blessings come through good *work*. We must be diligent and work at all times for God's glory. It is easy to become complacent and hope that gifts and blessings will fall from the sky. It is also easy to get caught is the "I deserve" frame of mind. But let's show up daily and give our best, make our best effort to do right in all things. Go above and beyond to glorify God and the rest will follow. That is right, blessing will follow.

Another scripture comes to mind

"Keep your lives free from the love of money and be content with what you have, because God has said, "Never will I leave you; never will I forsake you." (HEBREWS 13:5)

With gratitude for the blessings we have, and a desire to fulfill God's call on our lives, let's press forward to enjoy the full life we were created to have.

15

Whose body is it anyway?

DR. MARK

When we think of our physical body, do we ever consider who is the true owner? This is a big point of contention in the world today as evidenced by many movements that insinuate "This is my body, and I'll do with it what I want."

The questions for today are: is it your body, and is it your right to do anything you please with it?

Let's begin with 1 Corinthians 6:19-20: "Do you not know that your bodies are temples of the Holy Spirit, who is in You, whom you have received. You are not your own, you are bought with a price. Therefore, honor God with your bodies."

As believers, we are no longer owners of the physical body but instead, caretakers. If we truly believe this, we must go one step further and acknowledge what this responsibility really requires. There are thee tenets:
1. As caretakers, we must have due respect for the owner, who is God.
2. We do not have the right to destroy someone else's property.
3. For us to willingly decide to take control of someone else's property and in turn bring destruction, makes us thieves.

Let's examine a few of our cultural trends:
1. Culturally, there is a sense of worship of food. Unfortunately, this food is not food at all, and is disease-causing. What are these foods you ask? Here is a list: sugars, processed foods, fried foods, soda, MSG, bread, and grains.

2. Culturally, there is a belief that we need to "eat better." If we know what to do, and don't do it, is that willing abuse of God's temple? Indeed it is.
3. Culturally, we celebrate, give as rewards, and use as tools to bring crowds, the above mentioned inflammatory and disease-causing foods.

Introspection is the purest sense of self examination. Self-examination, when allowing God to illuminate and bring vision, is the greatest avenue towards repentance. Repentance, then, is to walk with a heart toward God and actions that follow.

16
Love and Gratitude

DR. MICHELE

We often hear about God's parental role and refer to Him as "God our Father."

Have I told my Heavenly Father how great He is and how much He has done, and continues to do, for me and my family? Surely, not enough times. That brings to mind the Hymn "How Great Thou Art" and also what the Psalmist says in Psalm 66:3.

"Say to God, 'How awesome are your deeds!'"

"O give thanks to the Lord for He is good, and His steadfast love endures forever...

Let them thank the Lord for His steadfast love, for His wonderful works to humankind!"
(PSALM 107)

This also makes me wonder, *Did I ever tell my folks how much their love of, and care for, me meant to me?* Surely, not enough times, because I took them for granted.

Now, when I ponder the Lord God as my Heavenly Parent, do I just take Him and what He does for granted?

Our Heavenly Parent created us in His image with the ability to recognize our potential and surroundings, then to respond appropriately, with love and with thanksgiving.

We all want to be appreciated and loved, to feel we are worth something, and needed. That's in our DNA. Our Heavenly Parent also wants us to show our love and gratitude to Him as well as to others, including our earthly parents. *How am I doing in that department?*

People need to love and be loved, to thank and be thanked, for wholeness of being. Jesus came to make us creatures of love and gratitude.

Thank you for being on this journey with us, through these readings. We love and appreciate you. We believe in you!

17
In Times of Trouble

DR. MICHELE

We know that in this life we will have troubles. Sometimes it seems as if the darkness will never end. But if we evaluate our *whole* lives we have assurance that God is always with us. He does not leave us or abandon us. In fact he gives us strength.

The following scripture is a reminder of the truth.

> "Fear not, for I am with you; be not dismayed, for I am your God; I will strengthen you, I will help you, I will uphold you with my righteous right hand." (Isaiah 41:10)

Being caught in fear is the devil's handiwork. We get spun out in that arena and forget our Sovereign God and the fact that he is our source of strength and will uphold us through the storms and place power in our wings. This power provides a robustness that can only come from above. For He turns all things together for the good.

In times of trouble worry not, use it as a time to press in to the One who knows the beginning from the end. He is our healing Father.

When things get overwhelming, another scripture comes to mind.

> "He who dwells in the shelter of the Most High will abide in the shadow of the Almighty. I will say to the Lord, "My refuge and my fortress, my God, in whom I trust." (Psalm 91:1-2)

Gods protection is like the protection of a parent over a child. Our children are wrapped in the shadow of our wings until they can stand on their own. As parents, that protective nature never goes away, no matter how old the child or how competent. It is the same with our heavenly Father. God wants us to always rely on him as our Father in heaven and master of healing and provision. He is our big daddy God in the sky.

Who wants to do this thing called life alone?

Our human will, will end up in failure before it is all said and done.

Mark and I will continue to press in to following biblical principles and relying heavily on our father in heaven to guide our steps. This is our hope and prayer for you always. We believe in you.

18

Creation from Connection

DR. MARK

Lord help me. I need more self-control!

Have you ever asked for more self-control? Certainly, I have. However, this question, as a believer, is wrought with many pitfalls and problems.

Before reacting one way or another, let's examine the following scripture very carefully:

Galatians 5:22-24: "but the fruit of the Spirit is love, joy, peace, forbearance, kindness, goodness, faithfulness, gentleness, and self-control. Against such things there is no law. Those who belong to Christ Jesus have crucified the flesh with is passions and desires."

As we know, a fruit doesn't become a fruit on its own. It simply becomes a fruit because it hangs on the vine which carries the nutrients and the DNA instruction for its creation. Said plainly, an apple doesn't have to work to become an apple; its creation is dependent upon its connection.

If the creation is dependent upon the connection, we see in the scripture the vital connection between us and the Holy Spirit. As a resident inside of our physical bodies, known as temples, the Holy Spirit is able to exhibit and magnify His own personal characteristics through us. What are those characteristics? That question has clearly been answered with the above scripture. It is simply the fruit of his presence. This is His character and nature.

Yet, therefore, when we ask for more self-control, as an example, we are intuitively saying that Holy Spirit's nature does not live in us. Or, perhaps, we have doubt or fear that God did not give it to us as He promised. That could not be further from the truth.

So, instead of asking for more self-control or even more faithfulness, let's simply begin to thank God that we have it in full measure and abundance.

With acknowledgement of His presence, and His subsequent nature, these attributes as listed in this scripture will begin to appear more visible, as a reflection of God's grace and goodness.

Yes, we will begin to see our lives becoming one big Holy Spirit fruit. How about them apples?

19
Written Stuff

DR. MICHELE

Despite ever-changing communications technology, families, schools, government officials, businesses, medical institutions, continue to use "written stuff" to carry out their activities. Indeed, this has been going on since ancient times.

And in your household, think about where you keep the title to your vehicles, and all those important documents. Yes, *written stuff*.

Reminds me of the purpose, promise, and importance of the written stuff we know as the Holy Scriptures. In this case, a sample from John 20:31:

"These are written so that you may come to believe that Jesus is the Christ (Messiah), the Son of God, and that through believing, you may have life through His Name."

Talk about the importance of written stuff! Those words create faith, which results in a life complete with love, peace, joy, hope, victorious power, and daily gracious care provided by Jesus, our Good Shepherd. And because of the inspired Word of God, we know we have a future with Him and life everlasting. Wow!

When we write things down in a journal or on a note pad, we have a reference for better accountability. If we drop accountability, we become drifters. We drift here and there with no definitive direction! God wants us to be clear on our direction! Most clearly he wants us to be devoted to a life centered on Him.

What's your direction and how do you keep on track? Maybe it should start with some written stuff. Logging your life gives you an account of where you have been and helps you see where you are going! (That's also why we encourage you to make notes about what God shows you in these daily readings.)

Make the written stuff, the story of your life, be something everyone wants to read.

It's easy to take from life the things that you want and then turn and run. It's easy to blow people off, and I'm sure you've had that painful experience. It's easy to say "I'll do it tomorrow." It's natural to procrastinate, but it leads to a life of rubble and confusion. I know wholeheartedly that I'm the only one that can change these things.

Mark and I have chosen to be accountable through written stuff: work notes, spiritual journals, training journals, personal logs, and more. At the end of the week in review, it gives a chance to see if there is complacency or determination.

It takes much more effort to stay in the game with accountability, however, it's worth it! If you get off the path, get back on.

20
Where is our Focus?

DR. MICHELE

Our God is a God of forgiveness and compassion. He is in control, yet He leaves us in charge. Giving us this reign allows for human mistakes and blunders. We often moan and complain about hardship we have created ourselves. As I have gotten older, I realize that it is not God who has forsaken and abandoned me, it is people.

Focus on pain, hurt, feelings of betrayal, and abandonment will always make for a heavy heart. This is the wrong focus.

Scripture reminds me, "For those who find me find life and receive favor from the Lord." (Proverbs 8:35)

Some days seem more daunting than others. The trials come, we lose focus, slip back into old habits and pathways of destruction. We must remember that we are the light of the world. Our focus should be on the One above.

Pleasing our Lord and Savior brings great reward. The reward is not always in our timing. It is in Gods timing. It is easy to get impatient and feel abandoned, alone, and grieved. We can ruminate on all of the bad and not even see the blessings.

How can we be the light with our focus on the wrong things? When that feeling of doom comes it is time to remember to cast our cares upon the Lord for He is mighty.

Being human comes with the temptations of the flesh that occur every day, sometimes multiple times a day. Being human comes with the consequences of mistakes. Thankfully we have a loving and forgiving Father. Every day a gut check is in order to evaluate who we serve.

Scripture reminds us: "For his anger lasts only a moment, but his favor lasts a lifetime; weeping may stay for the night, but rejoicing comes in the morning." (Psalm 30:5)

Today and always, strive to do what is good, right, and faithful and the reward will come.

21
Keys to receiving physical healing

DR. MARK

WHAT IS THE KEY TO EXPERIENCING PHYSICAL HEALING? IT IS CLEAR, by current disease statistics in our world, that sickness is becoming all too common. As a matter fact, according to the Centers for Disease Control and Prevention, we are growing sickness and disease conditions at a faster pace than the growth of the population. This, obviously, is not a sustainable process.

To that end, is there a key we're missing? Perhaps there is, and it may be found in the following passage from Mark chapter 10:

> "Now they came to Jericho. As He went out of Jericho with His disciples and a great multitude, blind Bartimaeus, the son of Timaeus, sat by the road begging. And when he heard that it was Jesus of Nazareth, he began to cry out and say, 'Jesus, Son of David, have mercy on me!' Then many warned him to be quiet; but he cried out all the more, 'Son of David, have mercy on me!'
>
> "So Jesus stood still and commanded him to be called. Then they called the blind man, saying to him, 'Be of good cheer. Rise, He is calling you.' And throwing aside his garment, he rose and came to Jesus.
>
> So Jesus answered and said to him, 'What do you want Me to do for you?'
>
> The blind man said to Him, 'Rabboni, that I may receive my sight.'

Then Jesus said to him, 'Go your way; your faith has made you well.' And immediately he received his sight and followed Jesus on the road."

Several keys here must be mentioned.
1. The blind man recognized Jesus and admitted there was a need. Many times, we do only one of the two. We recognize Jesus and fail to really understand the need. For example, what is the real need behind the healing process for type 2 diabetes? Is it for the process to go away, or for the mindset of lifestyle to change? It is the latter of course. That, in itself, is an adjustment and a true understanding of the need.
2. The blind man called to Jesus incessantly. He did not rely on the attention of anyone else. He realized Jesus was the key and nothing was going to stop him from seeking out the source of healing. Our healing does not come from doctors, instead, it comes from the Healer Himself, working through people at times, including doctors.
3. Once the disciples called for the blind man to come to Jesus, he had a decision to make. That decision was to listen, change positions, and move or wait for the healing to come to him. He chose the former, and by throwing off his cloak, he went to Jesus. We know at that moment Jesus granted him his healing.

All three points are important, but let's take a closer look at the third one. We have to be willing to change our current circumstances to receive healing. In this case, the blind man's coat signifies a heaviness, static, and weightiness in our current position. The cloak probably was dirty and moldy, and likely represents doing the same thing over and over again every day, getting no change in condition. He needed to change his perspective. He needed to be willing to move from where he was to where he needed to be. This may be a key to our physical healing in which we have been missing. We have been doing the same things and expecting different results.

To receive your healing, are you willing to change your mindset, your lifestyle, your food intake, and your very belief system as instructed by your culture? Are you willing to change positions and continue to learn?

Obviously, our lifestyle, especially the western lifestyle that permeates America (even America's church) is devastatingly dangerous. It needs to be changed, and this takes courage and willingness.

Can you be an agent of this change and walk in physical healing to bring glory to God and attention to His power? Don't wait on the group, and don't stay where you are. Get up, run to Jesus, change positions and perceptions, and receive your healing.

22

Sheer Love

DR. MICHELE

I's TIME FOR A MIND MASSAGE WITH THE GOOD WORD. *WE ARE PRECIOUS in our Father's eyes.*

"Because you are precious in My sight and honored, and because I love you, I will give men in return for you and peoples in exchange for your life." (ISAIAH 43:4)

Do you realize your worth to Abba Father?

He sent His Son to die for you.

He says in His word you are the apple of His eye. And He means it.

He has promised to protect you and care for you.

He knows your steps. Your steps have been ordered. So let's be obedient so we can enjoy His good plan. Why suffer when we don't have to. Trying to follow our own plan will lead to wreckage!

Scripture comes to mind.

> "Do this because you are a people set apart as holy to God, your God. God, your God, chose you out of all the people on Earth for himself as a cherished, personal treasure." (DEUTERONOMY 7:6-11)

Here's this verse again from The Message:

> "GOD wasn't attracted to you and didn't choose you because you were big and important—the fact is, there was almost nothing to you. He did it out of sheer love, keeping the promise he made to your ancestors. GOD stepped in and mightily bought you back out of that world of slavery, freed you from the iron grip of Pharaoh king of Egypt. Know this: GOD, your God, is God indeed, a God you can depend upon. He keeps his

covenant of loyal love with those who love him and observe his commandments for a thousand generations. But he also pays back those who hate him, pays them the wages of death; he isn't slow to pay them off—those who hate him, he pays right on time. So keep the command and the rules and regulations that I command you today. Do them."

Why would we cheat yourselves? Why would we think our own plan is best? God has plans for you. Dig in and stay the course!

"You have to live with Christ to know Him, and the longer you live with Him, the more you will admire and adore Him, and the more you will receive from Him, even grace for grace." (CHARLES H SPURGEON)

23
Walking Securely

DR. MICHELE

THIS PAST WEEK I WAS HAVING A CONVERSATION WITH A FRIEND ABOUT the definition of this noun: integrity. We pondered a while and begin to search out what that looks like in our lives. We agreed it is an important character trait.

Integrity means meeting one's responsibilities honestly and completely. A process has integrity if it works as it is intended to and fits into the larger system of which it is a part. I found myself reaching for the Bible (the basic instructions before leaving earth) to help my understanding.

> "Whoever walks in integrity walks securely, but he who makes his ways crooked will be found out." (PROVERBS 10:9 ESV)

This backs up the literal definition of integrity. We are to live a life meeting our responsibilities in truth and finish them. That is a goal to set for every day. It is so easy to get off course and abandon this principle. Life gets busy sometimes and before we know it our ways can get crooked. This can even relate to how we take care of our health.

When things get busy, our own lives can get set on the back burner. Left unchecked day after day, this can lead to physical destruction. We can get out of tune: physically, emotionally, intellectually, and spiritually.

> "The integrity of the upright guides them, but the crookedness of the treacherous destroys them." (PROVERBS 11:3 ESV)

Integrity is a guide. It is like a compass. A compass that we need to lean on at all times. Exercise this character trait and live by it ferociously.

"Better is a poor man who walks in his integrity than a rich man who is crooked in his ways." (Proverbs 28:6 ESV)

It is better to be poor and have integrity than be rich and crooked. God sees all. Mark and I aim to live with integrity every day and we will always be accountability partners to one another. We keep each other straight and on the narrow path. This is our hope and prayer for you also. May you live with integrity and right principles all the days of your life.

24
The Genetics of Diet

DR. MARK

Dr. Michele and I are experts in the field of nutrigenomics. That sounds like a complicated and difficult to comprehend science, which undoubtedly it is. We've studied many long hours to conceptually understand human genetics and its relationship with nutrition and environmental influence. Trust me, our studies continue this day and will continue for the rest of our lives.

That said, there is one factor that still blows our minds: human genetics has only evolved roughly 2% in the last 10,000 years. Now that's a long time!

How does this relate to scripture? Well let's go back to the time of Noah, which likely fits into this genetic timeframe in which we are referring. Here's our passage from Genesis 9:

> "So God blessed Noah and his sons, and said to them: 'Be fruitful and multiply, and fill the earth. And the fear of you and the dread of you shall be on every beast of the earth, on every bird of the air, on all that move on the earth, and on all the fish of the sea. They are given into your hand. Every moving thing that lives shall be food for you. I have given you all things, even as the green herbs.'"

After the flood, when Noah's ark landed on the mountain, Noah received specific instructions from God. We point out in these instructions that God clearly gave authority to Noah over creatures of the earth, birds of the air, and plants on the ground with the clear guidelines: these will *all* be food for you to eat. Noah was neither encouraged to be a vegetarian, nor was he encouraged to only eat meat. He was simply told to eat all these things that God had made.

Here's the point: if we have predominately the same genes that Noah had when he was given these instructions, and we know these genes are crafted for each of us by the personal hand of God, then these must be foods for us to eat to sustain the life of our bodies.

Keep in mind, food is instruction with information that makes our genes respond and express themselves. I won't get into the biochemistry and physiology here, but know that certain foods contain vital vitamins and minerals for optimal bodily function. Without these necessary elements, our body is destined to try to survive and run in a nutrient deficient environment.

So, let's do a little honest thinking. At the time in which Noah landed the ark, were there Twinkies, donuts, pizza, or soda? Of course not! They are simply the world's substitutes for what God made.

Please know that we present this information with love and hope to inspire a better understanding of God and His creation. We ask you to ask God to clarify His unique design for all of our lives and give us clear instructions on how are to care for the God-crafted personal vehicle and temple: the human body.

Take good care of your whole person today. We are for you!

25

More than Seasonal

DR. MICHELE

As Christians, we celebrate Easter, the resurrection of Jesus Christ. It's an annual seasonal celebration, and the highlight of the church calendar.

But we should celebrate each day, as they are God-given! This day is not to be taken for granted as if we are "owed" another day or another breath! Year 'round we need to keep our thoughts on the significance of the Resurrection. Every daybreak should remind us of Easter. Each morning we go from darkness to light.

As the day begins, we need the life-giving, victorious gifts of the resurrection to live right in a dark and wrong world. This life is tough, but by His grace we are healed! This Scripture comes to mind from Romans 6:4:

"As Christ was raised from the dead by the glory of the Father; so we too might walk in newness of life."

God's over-coming "glory power" demonstrated in the raising of Jesus from the dead, makes a glorious reality possible. Baptized believers may now live a daily-renewed life. How powerful! Another chance to let go of wretchedness and receive life.

Adventurers with a long journey, or a mountain to climb, know their daily need for food, clothing, shelter, and appropriate tools. Similarly, we Christians, have God's "backpack" provided for us on a daily basis.

The Bible points us to Jesus' resurrection and the empty tomb with the words, "He is not here. For He has been raised!" (Matt. 28:6). And "As Christ was raised from the dead by the glory of the Father; so we too might walk in the newness of life." (Romans 6:3-4)

That means every-day newness for each one of us! With this in mind, consider speaking this truth out loud:

"Because of Jesus' resurrection, I have all I need to live this day!"

Some days that does not seem possible! Some days are so ridden with man-made disaster! But God is right there, *every day*, with His heart for us and His hand reaching towards us!

Now, that's more than seasonal! Love and serve God with all your heart today, for He knows the beginning from the end.

26
Walk In The Spirit

DR. MICHELE

As each day goes by, the conversation comes up about peace. Why can't we all live in peace? Especially as we watch the drama going on around the world. It seems so easy to say, "Live in peace, be at peace, it's a choice" yet, it seems an impossible dream. Why?

Let's look at chapter 4 in the book of James.

> "What causes fights and quarrels among you? Don't they come from your desires that battle within you? You desire but do not have, so you kill. You covet but you cannot get what you want, so you quarrel and fight. You do not have because you do not ask God. When you ask, you do not receive, because you ask with wrong motives, that you may spend what you get on your pleasures."

Perhaps we must re-evaluate our motives. Battling the fleshly desires within can lend serious emotion that brings every wicked act, except peace. To make a conscious decision every day about motives is important to bring peace in our own lives. If each one of us lives at peace, we can spread peace, hope, and healing to the world.

We have to analyze if we are in step with the Spirit. If we get off track, the following scripture is a reference or compass to remind us just how far off track we are and helps us get back on the path of peace.

"But I say, walk by the Spirit, and you will not gratify the desires of the flesh. For the desires of the flesh are against the Spirit, and the desires of the Spirit are against the flesh, for these are opposed to each other, to keep you from doing the things you want to do. But if you are led by the Spirit, you are not under the law (of the flesh). Now the works of the flesh are evident: sexual immorality, impurity, sensuality, idolatry, sorcery, enmity, strife, jealousy, fits of anger, rivalries, dissensions, divisions, envy, drunkenness, orgies, and things like these. I warn you, as I warned you before, that those who do such things will not inherit the kingdom of God. But the fruit of the Spirit is love, joy, peace, patience, kindness, goodness, faithfulness, gentleness, self-control; against such things there is no law. Those who belong to Christ Jesus have crucified the flesh with its passions and desires." (GALATIANS 5:16-24)

This scripture sure speaks loudly. It is the acts of the flesh that drive us to war (most often the war that goes on inside of us). This war will drive us to partake in the multitude of negative things that keep our lives, and the world, in disarray if not corrected.

For today, and every day, let's evaluate our motives, evaluate if the works of the flesh are evident and working in our lives. If any are revealed, let's pray reverently that they are corrected immediately as we act consciously to intentionally maintain peace.

Our hope is for us to be beacons of hope for the world. May you live in peace.

27

What Drives our Choices?

DR. MARK

Some might wonder, "We're all going to die as that is our destiny. What do my choices matter?" Part of that statement is indeed true. But as believers, our purpose on this earth is to live every day in a way that exhibits excellent representation of the Kingdom of which we are citizens.

Much confusion comes from not considering what it truly means to *live* during this life on earth. Let's look at a couple of scriptures.

> "The thief does not come except to steal, and to kill, and to destroy. I have come that they may have life, and that they may have it more abundantly." (John 10:10)

> "I am the way, the truth, and the life. No one comes to the Father except through Me." (John 14:6)

In both of these verses, Jesus talks about giving us "life." What is this life? Is it life at our future destination in the Kingdom of heaven? Or is it life now, right here on earth?

The answer is *both*. We are to live today like we're going to live forever, while also considering today may be our last day on earth. Now that is a powerful concept!

We would submit to you that many people are making choices that willfully and highly likely shorten their life on this earth, which shortens their ability to fully exhibit God's plan for them. This is done with a mindset that may be only focused on reaching heaven but not focused on bringing heaven into earth now.

Jesus talked about both when he exhibited his model prayer which stated in part, "Thy Kingdom come, Thy will be done, on earth as it is in heaven."

That's right! We are supposed to live with the intent and purpose of bringing heaven into this earth, right now!

Each choice we make (pertaining to our physical, emotional, and spiritual lives) should be based on the reality that our choices affect our ability to fulfill God's purpose for us.

If we live intentionally reckless, expecting God to fix every willful mistake, we may be falling for the deceptive trap of self-centeredness, which may be described with the following mentality, "I'm going to do what I'm going to do to make me happy, since I'm going to die anyway."

Hopefully, this blog will spark new concepts in regard to your choices today. Choose life.

28
Spring has Sprung

DR. MICHELE

MARK AND I FELLOWSHIP WITH A GROUP OF SACRED FRIENDS ON A monthly basis. Lately, one of our friends has been too ill to join us. When I call him on the phone to include him, I ask, "What good words have you got for our meeting tomorrow evening?"

On a recent call he responded, "Spring is springing!"

I countered, "Don't you mean Spring has sprung?"

"No, Spring is springing, it's not here yet, he replied. "You see only signs of Spring. However, you can't say that Spring has sprung while winter remains with us. But, we do see signs of it being here soon."

His perspective gave me some thoughts about living the Christian life on our journey home to glory. You see, dear ones, we don't know when the Lord chooses to "pull the curtain on time" and usher in eternity, but we know of its certainty, because of what Jesus has done to make the "Spring time of eternity" a reality.

He wouldn't have come to just make life better for our "wintery" time on this planet. However, we can truthfully say (based on His promises) "Spring is springing" because signs surround us.

> *"Those whom God foreknew, He also predestined to be conformed to the likeness of His Son."* (ROMANS 8:29)

Here we see something of God's plan for us: "to be conformed" to His image takes a lifetime. We don't become like Jesus at the drop of a hat. However, day by day, in our walk with Jesus, signs indicate "Spring is springing."

Blossoms of Jesus' beauty and eternity appear, but they have not fully "sprung" yet.

So, our response to God's plan for our lives ought to find us following Jesus, living like Jesus, and loving like Jesus.

This we do as we spend daily time with Him in His life-changing Word, humble worship, and faithful in prayer. When He calls for our home-coming with Him in glory, these blossoms of His image within us will be in full bloom. Then, we can truly say "Spring has sprung!"

29
Toxic Fruits

DR. MICHELE

One of the counter fruits of the spirit is jealousy. Jealousy is a destructive personality trait. We all have to evaluate ourselves to eradicate this negative emotion. Jealousy is an often overwhelming feeling of insecurity about a potential loss or inequity in distribution of resources. The term is also used to describe a feeling associated with being possessive of another person, such as a partner or friend.

Jealous people are incredibly toxic because they have so much self-hate that they can't be happy for anyone around them. And typically, their jealousy comes out as judgment, criticism, or gossip. According to them, everyone else is awful, uncool, or lacking in some way.

Scripture comes to mind.

"Goliath looked David over and saw that he was little more than a boy, glowing with health and handsome, and he despised him."
(1 Samuel 17:42)

That is right, Goliath was jealous of the young man David was. Perhaps he was full of a lot of self hate. Perhaps he was worried about the potential loss of power and/or fame.

We all have Goliath' in our lives. We must diligently work to eliminate the feeling of defeat this can seed in our hearts. Here are a couple words of encouragement to defeat the demon of jealousy. You can apply these same things personally if you deal with the toxic emotion of jealousy.

1. Don't let anyone look down on you if because of your youth, wisdom, fitness level or status.

2. Don't let bullies intimidate you. This suppressive behavior can wound the spirit.
3. Work on your glow (in health). Walk in Godly wisdom always. Read the Bible daily (*Basic Instructions Before Leaving Earth*). Hope can always be found there.
4. Understand you will be despised by the systems (and people) of this world. Jesus was despised, betrayed, and hated by many. It did not stop him from loving and healing people.

Stand up with courage; God is bigger than any enemy!

30

Is there Comfort found in Sickness?

DR. MARK

Is THERE COMFORT FOUND IN SICKNESS? BEFORE YOU RESPOND (OR react) to this question, let me paint a picture for you:

You are a pastor. You routinely pray for people each Sunday during a time of ministry. You know that it's important and you certainly believe in the power of prayer.

You noticed that one particular parishioner, let's call her Bernice, routinely asks you for prayer for persistent numbness in her feet and mysterious non-healing wounds on her lower legs. She tells you the numbness is beginning to affect her balance and she is very concerned about infection.

You pray over her, agreeing for healing, week after week. However, Bernice continues to return with the same prayer request and no change in symptoms. Upon further discussion, you eventually find out that Bernice has a group of symptoms that point to type 2 diabetes. You also find out that she is routinely seeking doctor's care and they tell her repeatedly to avoid sugars, processed foods, grains, and other refined foods that are driving the current condition.

What would your specific prayer for Bernice be now? Did it change?

What is *healing* in this case? Is healing for the numbness to go away? The wounds to heal? Or, is your prayer that Bernice will be healed of type 2 diabetes?

It's clear that personal choices have contributed to Bernice's current condition. Based on that, our prayer should center on a change in mindset, leading to a change in choices.

It is very important to understand that changing mindset, and certain behavior, is extremely difficult, as we're talking about lifestyle. Could Bernice lose something by getting well? Perhaps she could lose your constant attention and prayers as her pastor? Would this make her happy or give her a letdown?

While this certainly isn't the case for everyone experiencing health challenges, there often exists a deception wrapped around finding comfort in the midst of an ongoing disease process. Remember, our enemy, is the master of telling us that diseases are only supposed to be *managed*. Jesus, however, exhibited complete healing and total remediation of disease processes.

Discern how to pray, be bold with instruction and encouragement, and understand that people need to be loved and experience true healing.

31
God's Favor

DR. MICHELE

Here are some scripture-based decrees and benedictions for God's favor to pray aloud in your secret place with God.

Dear Jesus,

Let me be satisfied with favor and filled with your blessing. (Deuteronomy 33:23)

I know you favor me because my enemies do not triumph over me. (Psalm 41:11)

Lord, be favorable unto my land. (Psalm 85:1)

Lord, grant me life and favor. (Job 10:12)

In your favor Lord, make my mountain stand strong. (Psalm 30:7)

Lord, I entreat your favor. (Psalm 45:12)

Lord, I entreat your favor with my whole heart. (Psalm 119:58)

Let your favor cause my horn to be exalted. (Psalm 89:17)

Lord, this is my set time for favor. (Psalm 102:13)

Remember me, O Lord, with the favor that you bring unto your children, and visit me with your salvation. (Psalm 106:4)

Let your favor be upon my life as a cloud of the latter rain. (Proverbs 16:15)

Let your beauty be upon my life, and let me be well favored. (Genesis 29:17)

I am highly favored. (Luke 1:28)

I am increasing in favor with God and man. I humble myself and receive more favor and grace in my life.

I will increase in wisdom knowledge and understanding, and I am increasing in favor.

My gifts make room for me and bring me before great people. (Proverbs 18:16)

Favor causes blessings to come to me, and through me.

32

Can I Actually Bless the Lord?

DR. MICHELE

YESTERDAY WAS A DAY OF CHALLENGE.

Sometimes challenges seem insurmountable. But today, is a new day and one to invite with a newness that brings light and joy to the world. On that note, I will reference Psalm 103 and its 1st verse:

"Bless the Lord O, my soul and all that is within me, bless His Holy Name!"

You mean I can actually BLESS the Lord? Indeed, I give Him a blessed gift whenever I want to talk with Him, worship Him, and pray to Him. Our loving Heavenly Father enjoys conversations with His children, and I am one of His kids. Don't parents appreciate when their children want to take time to talk to them, to show love and respect for them? For parents, that's a tremendously valuable gift!

As we acknowledge God for who He is and for what He has done, by worship, thanksgiving, and praise, we bless Him, for it reveals our faith in Him. You see, He's blessed in the fact that we trust Him. In addition, whenever we tell others about God's goodness and grace in Jesus Christ, He finds pleasure in and from us. Indeed, that blesses Him too.

Jesus said, "Truly, I tell you just as you did it to the least of these, who are members of My family, you did it to Me." (MATT. 25:40). That's a big thought, indeed! When we do what we can to help others in their need, we actually give Jesus a blessing.

We can bless the Lord in multiple ways. Give it thought and prayer. I'm sure you will discover other ways to bless our great and gracious God. Sometimes, it's just "showing up, taking the time to be in His awesome Presence blesses Him.

In all times, challenging times, joyous times, hurtful times, Mark and I show up to bless the Lord. That is our hope and prayer for you also. Show up and be the blessing, no matter the circumstance.

33
Have we Fired The Great Physician?

DR. MARK

THE TITLE OF TODAY'S READING MAY SURPRISE YOU. BUT WE ARE serious. Have we taken the great physician, terminated his role, and removed him from his position? There are over fifty biblical references to God being our healer.

As an example, let's dive into one verse making this reference:

> "And he said to them, doubtless you were quoting me this proverb, 'physician, heal yourself'. What we have heard you did at Capernaum, do you here in your hometown as well" (LUKE 4:23)

As we know, and as we clearly see, references to God being our great physician are pointed and direct. But, perhaps we need to revisit our own perception of our great physician. Do we go to Him first? Do we listen to His directives? Do we obey His commands?

To make these questions more illustrative, let's consider this scenario:

As a parent, your child comes to you and says their stomach is upset. After a few questions, you determine they ate something very unhealthy. You caution them not to eat that again.

The next day, your child returns with the same complaint. Again, you determine they ate the same pollution-filled, chemically-altered food. You admonish them and encourage them to stop the sickness-causing behavior.

Again, the following day, you guessed it, they repeated their poor choice. They did not listen to your warning. Now, they are sick, such that they require acute medical intervention.

Your love for that child does not diminish during this succession of events. You are grateful they came to you. However, you are grieved they didn't listen.

Our father God, the greatest of all physicians, tells us what to do, how to do it, what to eat, and what to stay away from to keep us healthy and well, all the days of our life.

Do we need medicine? Sometimes, yes. But to depend on someone wearing a white coat, as opposed to The One wearing a white robe, is the greatest of all absurdities.

Perhaps, we need give the great physician his job back.

34
Good Things from Bad

DR. MICHELE

MANY PEOPLE IN IRELAND, OUR COUNTRY, AND AROUND THE WORLD celebrate St. Patrick's Day, for the good this Patron Saint did.

This world changer of the fifth century was born to a British alderman with all the comforts wealth offers. Yet he became a slave in Ireland. How did that happen? Well, Irish chieftains secured slaves through rogue slave traders, who snatched healthy youth wherever opportunity presented itself. After six years of slavery, Patrick escaped and went back home to Britain.

Sometimes, when bad things happen, good can result. Rather than curse God, or his Irish slave masters, after a conversion experience with Christ, he reflected on what he should do with his life. He sought the Lord's guidance and soon found himself studying theology, mainly in France, and then felt a call to become a missionary.

Interestingly, Patrick had fallen in love with the Irish people when enslaved there; so to Ulster, Ireland he went. Amazing, wouldn't you say? One never knows what plans the Lord has for us, nor where His Spirit chooses to send us. He has plans and places for all of us. It is up to each of us to seek God's guidance and be willing to go and do whatever the Lord lays on our hearts.

In my thinking, the Scripture that describes best the message St. Patrick shared with the Irish people, the Apostle Peter used on the day of Pentecost.

> *"Peter said to them, 'Repent, and every one of you be baptized in the Name of Jesus Christ for the remission of sins, and you will receive*

the gift of the Holy Spirit, for the promise is to you and your children."
(ACTS 2:38-39)

    You see, St. Patrick's message centered on the Cross and what Jesus did for individuals, parents, and children. The Irish honor Patrick for always including their children. The Irish claim that the shamrock plant best describes the Gospel message. The plant resembles a three leaf clover, with one leaf on top and two on each side of the stem. The three together representing the Father, Son, and Holy Spirit. The positioning of the leaves on the stem forms a cross-like appearance.

    The message of St. Patrick centered on Christ, the crucified One, who proved God's love for each, and who gives His Spirit to all. Mark and I seek to know God's will for us each day we live, and we believe that's your prayer and desire also.

35

Pray and Resist

DR. MICHELE

This scripture resonates as I reflect on how Jesus handled tough situations, even when those around Him fell into temptation

> "Then they came to a place which was named Gethsemane; and He said to His disciples, 'Sit here while I pray.' And He took Peter, James, and John with Him, and He began to be troubled and deeply distressed. Then He said to them, 'My soul is exceedingly sorrowful, even to death. Stay here and watch.' He went a little farther, and fell on the ground, and prayed that if it were possible, the hour might pass from Him. And He said, 'Abba, Father, all things are possible for You. Take this cup away from Me; nevertheless, not what I will, but what You will.' Then He came and found them sleeping, and said to Peter, 'Simon, are you sleeping? Could you not watch one hour? Watch and pray, lest you enter into temptation. The spirit indeed is willing, but the flesh is weak.'"
> (Mark 14:32-38 NKJV)

Today, may we continue to pray and resist temptation, so we can continue to be the light and life in this world. It is far to easy to fall, not only fall asleep, but into the hands of temptation that will ruin the life we are given to live.

May we go a little farther, dig a little deeper, even when circumstances seem out of control. When our soul gets sorrowful and we get overwhelmed, may we not fall into the darkness that so readily seeks to kill, steal, and destroy.

Remember to go a little farther, press in and pray and do not be wooed by the temptations that lead only to destruction.

God is our Pillar and Strength. With His help, may you also be a pillar of hope and strength, one day at a time.

36

Looking up

DR. MICHELE

Walking through this thing called life, days come and go, the tides and waves rise and fall, the brightest of days and the darkest of nights are all ebbing and flowing, just like the seasons. It is easy to become complacent, distracted and even uninterested in living in a righteous manner.

However, scripture comes to mind:

"My son, do not forget my teaching, but let your heart keep my commandments, for length of days and years of life and peace they will add to you. Let not steadfast love and faithfulness forsake you; bind them around your neck; write them on the tablet of your heart. So you will find favor and good success in the sight of God and man." (Proverbs 3:1-4)

Keeping Gods commandments brings peace, length of days, and years of life. Who does not want that? Even in the rough times, being steadfast is worth it. Let's write love and faithfulness on our hearts and bind them like jewels around our necks!

Another scripture comes to mind.

"He always comes alongside us to comfort us in every suffering so that we can come alongside those who are in any painful trial." (2 Corinthians 1:4)

Even in our most painful moments he will be there. Instead of looking down, let's look up to our Father who holds us dear. He does not forget us or forsake us. He remains true. *He* is our strength and our fortress, not people, gold, goods, or fame.

One more scripture:

"Trust in the Lord with all your heart, and do not lean on your own understanding. In all your ways acknowledge him, and he will make straight your paths. Be not wise in your own eyes; fear the Lord and turn away from evil. It will be healing to your flesh and refreshment to your bones." (PROVERBS 3:5-8)

This is what Mark and I aim to do every day. We trust in the Lord with all of our might and lean not on our own understanding. God heals the broken hearted and gives the strength needed to carry on.

This is our hope for you also! Be steadfast in your ways and keep hope and faith in your heart!

37
Is the "Daniel Fast" Biblical?

DR. MARK

This is a very profound question that is rarely (if ever) asked. Let's dive in to the Word of God and see if we can determine the answer:

First let's set up the back story. Jehoiakim was still king of Judah when Daniel and others were taken captive by the king of Babylon in 605 BC. During Daniel's first years in Babylon, things did not get better back in Judah. Daniel and his friends watched as many other Jews eventually joined them in this foreign city.

Meanwhile, Daniel and the Jewish captives in Babylon had to make the best of their new lives. Daniel and other young men were chosen to live at the palace and be educated. Nebuchadnezzar had conquered many nations besides Judah, and he was gathering the best minds to be trained as helpers in his government. The king planned a three-year course of study for these young men. Daniel had the opportunity to acquire the best possible education of the day. The Babylonians had knowledge of math and astronomy, as well as medicine. Chemistry and metallurgy were established sciences of Daniel's time; theology and philosophy would also have been included.

The man in charge of the students gave them Babylonian names. "Daniel" was Hebrew for "my judge is God." His new name, "Belteshazzar" meant "protect his life" and honored a Babylonian god. The food and wine assigned to the young men from the king's table were probably very rich, luxurious, rare foods that only the wealthy could afford. But the problem with the king's food and wine was that it had all been involved in worship ceremonies to heathen idols, and anyone who ate it was honoring the idol. Also, God had given the Hebrews strict laws about food. Pork and some other kinds of meat were not to be eaten at all, and when cattle or sheep were killed, the blood was to be carefully drained from them. These rules were not followed in Babylon. Daniel believed he would be defiled if he did not keep God's laws.

The man in charge of the young scholars considered Daniel's refusal to eat the king's food. However, the overseer was afraid to disobey the king. What if he gave the Hebrew boys some other kind of food, and then they were not so strong and handsome as the rest of the students? Then the king might be angry and cut off the head of the man who disobeyed him.

Daniel suggested a ten-day test. The Hebrew boys would eat vegetables and drink water instead of sharing the king's food and wine. The man agreed to try it. If the boys became weaker in ten days, then he would insist that they eat what the king ordered. The test proved that the Hebrews' diet was best, so it was continued.

God wanted these Hebrew boys to be His witnesses in Babylon. He helped them become the best of the students. To Daniel, God gave a special ability to understand the messages that He sometimes gave in dreams. The king himself gave the final examination at the end of the three years of training. He found that the Hebrew boys not only were the best of the students, but also were even wiser than the great scholars of Babylon. Daniel stayed in Babylon the rest of his life and grew to be an old man.

Daniel knew that his body was a gift from God. He wanted to take care of it and follow God's instructions. The New Testament does not contain specific food commands. Still, the principal of caring for the bodies that God gave us is clear. 1 Corinthians 6:19-20 talks about the fact that our body is a temple for Holy Spirit. We are to honor God with our bodies.

Therefore, Daniel's decision not to defile his body, but to instead consume health-giving foods, was permanent, not temporary. Hence, the answer to the original question is: there is *not* a biblically-derived "Daniel fast." Instead, there is a biblically described courageous decision by a young man to eat life-giving foods every day, even if it cost him his life.

38
A Real Boost

DR. MICHELE

I just came across these two verses from Psalm 118 that sparked my thinking:

"With the Lord on my side, I will not fear. What can mortals do to me? The Lord is on my side to help me." (Psalm 118:6-7)

Throughout life, we find ourselves taking sides with this or that team, with this or that discussion, with this or that political group, with this or that expression of Christianity, and with this or that particular person. So, taking sides seems to be a very familiar, normal, and important function of human life. The concern of the above verses appears to be whether or not the Lord is on our side.

The psalmist gives reasons for having the Lord on our side: "I will not fear" and "The Lord is on my side to help me."

Life's events can spawn fear, worry, and anxiety. With the Lord on my side, I keep fear from spoiling my days. Experiencing all of the difficulties of daily living, I find comfort knowing, that I receive help when the Lord is by my side.

Some people get their biggest physical "boost" from various drinks or foods, but for our mental and spiritual energy, nothing offers the "boost" that our God provides by the empowering of the Holy Spirit.

That's why Jesus came, so God would be on our side and we would be on His! Ponder this today. Jesus gave His life in order that we may enjoy God being on our side, and receive life's biggest "boost"!

39

On Earth, as it is in Heaven

DR. MICHELE

"Greater is He that is in you than he that is in the world." I heard these Bible words spoken on a radio broadcast today. Wow, that resonates with one of my favorite scriptures:

> "You, dear children, are from God and have overcome them, because the one who is in you is greater than the one who is in the world. They are from the world and therefore speak from the viewpoint of the world, and the world listens to them. We are from God, and whoever knows God listens to us; but whoever is not from God does not listen to us. This is how we recognize the Spirit of truth and the spirit of falsehood." (1 John 4:4-6 NIV)

Every day we have to use discernment to reveal if we are following Godly principles or worldly principles. It is easy to get pulled in the wrong direction if we are not on the lookout for false prophets and false ideas.

So much fear, division, and suppression is happening in our world today. These things are not of God. How do we fall for such traps? We unplug from what feeds us, the Living Word, the Holy Testament, the book of Truth named the Bible.

Mark and I find that the Bible is the best compass for navigating our time on earth. It keeps us close to the plans God has for us and away from the worlds plans. In fact, another scripture comes to mind:

> "'For I know the plans I have for you,' declares the Lord, 'plans to prosper you and not to harm you, plans to give you hope and a future.'" (Jeremiah 29:11 NIV)

If we are caught up in the wrong plans, God's plans can get delayed, unheard, and completely disheveled. This scripture does not mean that blessing shows up without effort. We have to apply ourselves to experience the fruit of our labor. That is what Mark and I do every day and will continue to do. We put in the work.

Our focus is on Godly principles, spending time in the Word and listening to God's voice. We make a concerted effort to turn off the world's voice, the voice of evil and division. We then put action to the plans God lays out before us. May people see God and experience God in us, and may He receive all the glory.

This is our hope and prayer for you also. Lead your life from Godly principles. If we all do this, the world can become much more like heaven.

40
Power Tools

DR. MICHELE

You've heard the expression, "We've come a long way, baby!"

Think about the ol' timers of centuries ago and what few tools they had to work with. Now, our homes and vehicles are full of tools. Webster defines "tool" as "an instrument designed to accomplish a task."

With that definition, even our phones can be classified as tools. Think of our smart phones, for a moment. They enable not just conversation, business transactions, and complex calculations, video viewing, and even step-by-step navigation. But every tool, from a hammer to a computer, requires a power source.

I'm reminded of Jesus words to His disciples, which includes you and me!

> "You shall receive power when the Holy Spirit comes upon you, and you shall be My witnesses in Jerusalem, in all Judea and Samaria, and to the ends of the earth!" (ACTS 1:8)

Imagine, ever since the first New Testament Pentecost, people transformed by the Holy Spirit have been empowered to be witnesses and make disciples. The Spirit not only energized them, but gave them words about Christ's life-transforming power, as scripture teaches:

> "... the Gospel. It is the power of God to salvation to everyone who believes." (ROMANS 1:8)

With these truths in mind, we pray that you receive more of this Holy Spirit power to please God and impact other people with the love of God. Here's what the Apostle Paul prayed when writing to the Church is Ephesus:

> *"I pray that according to the riches of His glory, He may grant that you may be strengthened in your inner being with power though His Spirit."* (EPHESIANS 3:16)

Receive a fresh charge of God's love and power right now. What a great tool!

41
Why Do We Fear?

DR. MICHELE

WHAT A BEAUTIFUL DAY! THIS IS THE DAY THAT THE LORD HAS MADE.

God has said "Never will I leave you, never will I forsake you."
(HEBREWS 13: 5-6)

We say with confidence, "the Lord is my helper and I will not be afraid." Why do we fear then? Ever? Why do we dampen our bright light?

Life can get hard sometimes, and can feel as if one is walking through the desert. It is human nature to become afraid that the dry times will never end. There's a temptation to *fear* dying of "dehydration" whether that comes from the lack of water, lack of work, lack of health, lack of finances, or lack of relationships.

Psalms 89:15-16 reminds us: "Happy are those who hear the joyful call to worship, for they will walk in the light of your presence Lord."

If we are living in fear can we hear the joyful call to worship? Can we hear anything at all except the negative voice in our heads?

We must stop the wasteland of the dark mind. The dark mind casts negativity on the present. The present is the only time we have. We cannot make a joyful noise while living in fear!

Don't just shine your light when things are right or seem right. Be the light. Always. In the most trying times, shine the brightest. This is the true witness of what God has done, is doing, and will do in the future.

Why do we worry? Jesus told us clearly that God watches the smallest birds, and cares for us so much more. We are his children, God is our father, and He keeps his promises.

"God is able to provide you with every blessing in abundance, so that having all sufficiency in all things at all times, you may abound in every good work." (2 Corinthians 9:8)

Please note the word. "work" in the verse above. God provides graciously so we can do our part. If you lack finances, work on improving them. If you are hurting, seek good counsel. If you're alone, find community and be a friend to someone who needs encouragement. If you are not well, seek health professionals to help you heal.

Shine bright as you step out and step up into your full potential. Water will pour over you when you dig the well. Continue to shine your light into every dark space. Let's squelch the dehydration of darkness and live to our full potential as we are designed!

42
The Second Secret to Resilience

DR. MARK

IN A PREVIOUS READING, WE FOCUSED ON THE CONCEPT OF FEAR AND how it can drive our physiological systems *away* from our God-given capacity to fight disease, as well as pathogenic bacteria or virus. Our thinking, beliefs, and conversation can shape this process.

Right now, let's focus on another major cause of a body's inability to have an effective immune system. This is a greater pandemic than coronavirus, and it's known as obesity, or said another way, excess fatness. Please understand, this has nothing to do with weight but rather excess fat tissue and decline of muscle tissue. (Body fat percentage of women should range between 18 and 28%. Men should range between 10 and 20%. Do you know your body fat percentage?)

Obesity rates have been climbing steadily for the last forty years. This began with the perpetual consumption of non-foods—those that are heavily processed, filled with sugar, genetically modified, and depleted of nutrients. As recently as the late 1970s, statistics revealed only one state out of fifty in the United States had an obesity rate of greater than 10%. After the introduction of the food pyramid, which drove the production of non-foods, it took only eleven years for forty-nine states' rates to cross 10%. Sadly, many states have surpassed the 50% threshold, for adults and children.)

We've all heard the media highlight the many deaths created by the coronavirus outbreak. This breaks my heart. And it's heartbreaking to also know that preventable factors contribute heavily, as proven statistically, to the deaths related to coronavirus infection. These include hypertension, cardiovascular disease, type-two diabetes, and obesity.

Let's understand that the vast majority, up to 90% of these conditions, are self-driven and chosen based on lifestyle. In other words, God did not create us to become hypertensive, cardiovascular-disease-filled, and obese humans that struggle to simply exist.

Dr. Michele and I are grateful for modern advances in medicine. However, can you imagine what we could do to improve our health if we simply took care of our temples?

As the Bible says: "But you are a chosen generation, a royal priesthood, a holy nation, His own special people, that you may proclaim the praises of Him who called you out of darkness into His marvelous light." (1 Peter 2:9)

If we are part of the priesthood, we are then called to act as priests. Priests, in the Old Testament, were required to care for the temple to ensure it was functioning and supplied accordingly. Today, we are still called to perform these duties with the temple. However, our temple today is not made of stone, jewels, and linen. It is made of flesh, bone, blood, and multiple organ systems that are miraculously and meticulously created by the very hands of God.

Perhaps the greatest cure for the coronavirus would be a complete repentance for our destructive, self indulgent, gluttonous behavior that had driven the destruction of our temples.

God is able to restore, rebuild, and reconstruct those things which are broken, if we humbly submit all our our lives, including our lifestyle, to Him. Just take one step today in the right direction.

43
The Enjoyment of God's Love

DR. MICHELE

Recently, this verse of Scripture came to my attention, provoking much thought:

> *"Who will separate us from the love of Christ? Will hardship, or distress, or persecution, or peril, or sword?* (Romans 8:35)

Not only "who" but "what" can separate us from God's love? From God's point of view, *nothing*! Another verse in that same context underscores the Lord's promise to us, and all because of Gods love.

> *"No, in all these things, we are more than conquerors through Him who loved us. For I am convinced that neither death, nor life, nor angels, nor rulers, nor powers, nor height, nor depth, nor anything else in all creation will be able to separate us from the Love of God in Christ Jesus our Lord."* (Romans 8:37-39)

Our heavenly Father won't stop loving us no matter what. Can we do something whereby we can't enjoy God's love?

With that question we must admit the possibility. So, another related question comes to mind, "Am I living in the enjoyment of God's love made possible by Jesus?"

Think about it. Well, I suppose that whenever I do what He doesn't approve of, I barricade the flow of His perfect love coming my way.

Praise God that it's always coming my way, even though I may block it due to my foolishness. "And praise God that His mercy endures forever, so I can get back on the narrow road.

Thought, word, and deed must always be attended to. In this life it's not easy. All the fleshly matters cause moment to moment temptation!

Mark and I sincerely try to avoid blocking the wonderful experience of God's love, though, at times, we do so. Still, His love keeps coming in the expression of forgiveness and other blessings of His marvelous grace.

We pray and trust that your thoughts move in that same direction today. Oh! what a loving God we have! What a Savior!

44
Lost and Found

DR. MICHELE

OUR LIVES SUFFER MANY KINDS OF LOSSES. LOSING SOMETHING, OR someone, can be devastating. But, finding something lost can bring much joy. Pondering such thoughts caused me to reflect on a parable of Jesus:

> "What woman having ten silver coins, if she loses one of them, does not light a lamp, sweep the house, and search carefully until she finds it? When she has found it, she calls together her friends and neighbors, saying: 'Rejoice with me for I have found the coin that I had lost!' Just so, I tell you, there is joy in the presence of the angels of God over one sinner that repents." (LUKE 15:8-10)

Recently I lost track of my key chain. How quickly frustrated and worried I became when not finding them in my pocket or purse. Just then, my doorbell rang. As I opened the front door, there was my neighbor, smiling, with my keys in her hand. "Could these be yours by any chance?"

Immediately, joy washed over my wearisome and worried heart! I had simply dropped them on the way into the house . Thank God for honest neighbors! Thank God for those who continue to live an honest and righteous life dedicated to serving others!

If you've ever lost something and then found it, you know what I'm talking about. Jesus relates the loss of just one physical item (and frantic search for it) to one sinner "found" for the Kingdom, and what joy this brings to the Heavenly Host and God Himself.

This story makes me think about priorities. I know where Christ's priorities are: He died so the lost (you and me) could be "found." And whenever just one sinner joins the Kingdom all of the angels express the priorities of heaven. They rejoiced when I was found! They rejoiced when you were found! How amazing is this? With Jesus, each and every sinner is worth His death on the *old rugged cross*!

How about our other priorities, related to the physical or spiritual realms? Do I care about family and others who may be lost, outside the Kingdom? If the answer is yes, how devoted are we?

Today let's prayerfully consider how to put our priorities in proper order."First things first!" Jesus loves you and so do we!

45
Builders and Destroyers

DR. MARK

As you walk the narrow road, and "feed" on God's Word to build your faith, let's consider clear ways to build our physical health.

Our immune system is one of the most extraordinary defense mechanisms ever created. Straight from the hand of God, this effective war machine is able to defend our bodies from threats both inside and outside. Simply put, if anything gets in or on your body with the intent on creating harm, your system is equipped with the ability to kill, neutralize, and disable the threat. Further, this extraordinary system has the ability to adapt to changing environments by creating new antibodies.

Here are a few choices that will prepare our immune system to do an amazing job.

1. Consume real foods. These include well-sourced proteins, quality fats, and organic fruits and vegetables.
2. Get sufficient sleep. 7 to 9 hours is required each night.
3. Effectively manage stress. This involves finding balance in life between stress inducing events and relaxation inducing events.
4. Exercise is critical. We all need a minimum of 150 minutes per week of dedicated activity. One can easily begin with a walking program.
5. The following supplements should be taken: zinc, vitamin C, vitamin D, omega three fatty acids, and magnesium. Others are important as well, but it is best to start with these. (See the back of this book for a special discount in our store.)

Where do you stand and where do you need to improve?

These are all very doable, right? Remember that our physical health impacts our mental and spiritual health. And when our bodies stop, our ministry stops.

46
Letters from God

DR. MICHELE

Recently, Mark and I received an encouraging letter from someone who has been a friend for a long time. I'm sure that you have also appreciated getting encouraging mail from time to time.

Ever thought about God's mail service? His letters to us? Really, that's what the whole Bible is about, our loving heavenly Father's letters for uplifting inspiration.

All of the Bible comes from the Lord, but He has used all kinds of different servants ("mail men") to do the writing. Some of these came from the pen of those who wrote specific letters, such as Peter, whose second letter I highly recommend for meditation today.

As you read those three chapters of 2 Peter, think of God writing a letter to you personally and pray for His Spirit to enlighten you into its meaning. To me, it's full of some great "stuff" for life today.

For example, note this verse from 2 Peter 1:20, that deals with God's mail system. "First you must understand this, that no Scripture is a matter of one's own interpretation, because no prophecy ever comes by human will, but men and women moved by the Holy Spirit spoke from God." (2 Peter 1:20)

Mark I have been reading these letters from God before and throughout our married life. They've kept us in touch and in tune with the Lord these many years, and we pray and trust that they will serve the same purpose for you also!

47
Words from Grandpa

DR. MICHELE

As a child, my Grandpa used to provide encouragement with scripture when fear was trying to run our lives. One of his favorite scriptures that rings in my head (and is reinforced by the soft, sweet voice of my husband) is:

"For God hath not given us the spirit of fear; but of power, and of love, and of a sound mind." (2 Timothy 1:7 KJV)

That truth is not always easy to grasp in today's society and in a fallen world. My grandfather wrote the following poem that I keep in the front cover of my Bible. Take a read and be encouraged.

One day I sought to find something
That would to myself great satisfaction bring.
So, I turned to the world's abundance of pleasure,
Thinking to find it there in the fullness of measure.

But, I was mistaken as I found out soon,
That the world can give only sorrow and gloom.
My mind is troubled, I cannot sleep;
For I know I have gone into sin real deep.

What can I do, is it now too late,
To get release from this sad state?
In my condition will even the Lord
Speak to me with just one kind word?

Then, as I laid one night on my bed,
There came a sweet voice to me and said,
You still may have this satisfaction,
If you come to Calvary's mountain.

For there I shed on that cruel tree,
All My blood that you may be,
Cleansed from sin and then receive
Eternal life which I freely give.

Thanks, dear Lord, I'll come today,
That I might walk the narrow way;
For now I know that then I'll find,
Wonderful peace for my troubled mind.

Listen, dear friends, who do not know,
Of this kind Savior, who loves us so…
Accept Him today and live for Him; and,
The pleasures of this world will grow wondrously dim.

Jesus will satisfy, you can't go wrong;
And, if you but accept you'll join the throng
That tell of this wonderful, wonderful Lord,
Who gives life eternal, according to His Word.

Grandpa spoke of the narrow road, and we know that very few find it. Be encouraged as you read this scripture in The Message:

"I don't know about you, but I'm running hard for the finish line. I'm giving it everything I've got. No sloppy living for me! I'm staying alert and in top condition. I'm not going to get caught napping, telling everyone else all about it and then missing out myself." (1 Corinthians 9:26-27 msg)

Notice the "no sloppy living" phrase! We can all improve today! Obedience to God's Word is key.

Live long, live strong! Love and fear cannot exist in the same breath!

48
In The Beginning

DR. MARK

"In the beginning, God."

If we truly believe God, we must also believe His Word is true. If we believe even one word is false, we must also believe all is false. Now, if that matter is settled, let's proceed with some of His Word laid out in the beginning, in the first chapter of Genesis.

"So God created man in His own image; in the image of God He created him; male and female He created them. Then God blessed them, and God said to them, "Be fruitful and multiply; fill the earth and subdue it; have dominion over the fish of the sea, over the birds of the air, and over every living thing that moves on the earth." And God said, "See, I have given you every herb that yields seed which is on the face of all the earth, and every tree whose fruit yields seed; to you it shall be for food."

When we unwrap this scripture, we find these truths:

We are created in the image of God. His image is perfect. So, we are perfectly created, not lacking anything.

God provided food grown from the earth to sustain his creation. He also created the appetite toward that food which he created.

God gave us dominion (authority) over the earth, which would include the physical body which was created from the earth.

Therefore, if God made us perfect and provided all we need, we do not need to live in fear about sickness or disease. Sickness and fear of death or virus does not need to be our focus. Instead, let's focus on living a life of fullness in God. Additionally, if what we put in our mouths (the food we eat and drink) does not meet the criteria of God's intent (coming from the earth in its original packaging) then we are disobedient to His provision.

As we know, the recent pandemic has been perpetuated by our failure to follow these simple truths. But it has shown us our weaknesses—spiritually, emotionally, and physically. Let's take the following inventory:

Do I view my life as lacking anything? (Do I really think God made my immune system to be poor and inadequate?)

Am I truly feeding my body correctly? (Do I repeatedly ingest food that is not food at all?

Am I sedentary? (Do I sit too much?)

Have I allowed God to really have authority in the renewal of my mind? (Do I speak and mimic concepts that do not line up with God's truth?)

Taking inventory and revisiting foundational truth brings direction and confidence in our lives. This confidence, which is from God and in God, yields a life that shines like the brightest star in the darkest night. Let's all shine brighter today.

49
Talking and Listening

DR. MICHELE

The other day at the airport I watched a young couple having a conversation. (I was not trying to eavesdrop, yet I couldn't help but notice.) One person dominated the conversation and even spoke what they assumed was the mind of the other.

It was as if only one person was constantly talking, and no one was listening. The relationship seemed disconnected.

I had to stop and evaluate this in my own life. Do I talk to much? How well do I listen? Should I ask better questions? Am I present to the people who talk to me? Do I sit and listen disconnected?

When we talk constantly we miss listening. When we don't listen we miss building relationship.

Building a relationship requires effective communication and understanding.

If we are not listening, we can't be fully present to build deep relationships. We have to balance talking and listening in order to build healthy relationships, and we need to be fully present!

This verse quickened me to evaluate how much I run my rattle trap and if I am present when I am listening.

"Let every man be swift to hear, slow to speak, slow to wrath."
(James 1:19)

Those skilled in relationships seek first to understand (listen and ask questions to clarify) before they seek to be understood. We are given two ears and one mouth for a reason.

Moving forward I'll begin to listen more and ask more questions to ensure I am hearing what is intended to be communicated. I'll even repeat back, "I am hearing you say… Is that what you are saying?" I'll practice being fully present!

I am confident the outcome will be positive breakthrough in relationships. Let's aim to talk less and listen more. Let's hear what each other has to say. Take a pause in between our sentences to listen and be engaged. This will shift our listening to a place of being present to another.

It is a wonderful thing to be heard. It's also wonderful to hear the wonders of the lives of those we love!

50
God's Book of Love

DR. MICHELE

Greetings this beautiful day! How do I know it's a beautiful day?

God's grace and peace is upon us today, all the days of our lives!

I came across this passage of Scripture that sparked some deep thoughts:

> *"In Your book were written all the days that were formed for me, when none of them yet existed. How weighty to me are Your thoughts, O God! How vast is the sum of them! I try to count them, they are more than the sand."* (Psalm 139:17-18)

Makes me wonder, *You mean, God maintains a book about me?* He keeps track of me — who I am and what I do?

Does that mean I must have some worth, and also, am I accountable to Him?

Good questions to consider for each of us! But, there's more to this passage:

"How weighty to me are Your thoughts."

How about that? God thinks about me and you! Can you imagine His thoughts? Could they be filled with moments of love, just like the memory books that parents keep? Ponder this Scripture:

> *"In this is love, not that we loved God, but that He loved us and sent His Son to be the atoning sacrifice for our sins... God is love and those who abide in love abide in God, and God abides in them."* (1 John 4:10, 16)

God's book about us can rightfully be referred to as God's Love Book, and it's filled with loving thoughts. Though I admit that I disappoint my Savior from time to time, He still maintains His thoughts about us. Indeed, God *is* love!

Now let's ponder, *What are my thoughts about loving my Heavenly Father, and my Savior, Jesus?*

51
Capturing Your Attention

DR. MICHELE

What gets your attention? I have been writing these posts for over four years now, every Saturday or Sunday! I have committed to carry on a legacy of two special people that gave me my spiritual wings! The first my mother who taught me to pray every day and read the Bible (basic instructions before leaving earth). Secondly my grand father! My grandfather blessed the lives of many with his faithful weekly messages! I continue to write for his legacy as well.

This past weekend something got my attention. I got lured away educating my mind in an exotic place with Mark Sherwood and whoops…… I forgot to write. Here I go to stay on track with an unbroken commitment that challenges me to stay focused! Stay with me!

With all of the attractive advertising and alluring gimmicks used, really, what gets your/my attention? Besides the world of business, marketing, sports, arts/crafts, music, theater, etc. begging for a look and listen, our great and loving heavenly Father, tries to get our attention, also. These verses focus on that desire of His:

> "Now then, My sons, listen to Me; pay attention to what I have to say!" (Proverbs 7:24)

> "We must pay greater attention to what we have heard, so that we do not drift away from it." (Hebrews 2:1)

> "… I called, but you did not answer. I spoke and you did not listen. You did evil in My sight and chose what displeases Me." (Isaiah 65:12b)

Glamorous advertising that brings us into an auto dealership, or any high-priced merchant's facility, might keep us from realizing what's at stake in purchasing their expensive products. A person may get in over their head by making a deal that looks too good to pass up. So, we need to be careful of who and what gets our attention in many areas of life. It could cost us dearly!

Listening and paying close attention to what the Lord our God has to say, and do, for us, will do us well when we respond positively.

Not paying attention, can really cost us. Think of the Holy Spirit as the Heavenly "salesman." He works on the inside to get our attention. Doing that, He shows us what priceless "products" God offers. The Spirit of God does not, nor will he ever, be deceptive regarding what God promises.

Yes, there is a personal cost! We "trade in" our old self to Jesus, and get a new self back. *Such a deal you can't refuse!*

Jesus offers us the best "deal" for life, which we experience when we complete the transaction, which demands the faith of our hearts. His offer of life also includes: complete acceptance, perfect love, amazing grace, genuine hope, comforting peace, sufficient power for each day's demands, victorious living, citizenship in God's eternal Kingdom, and more.

Let these truths capture your full attention today.

52
Dead Silence

DR. MARK

"Dead silence" is how we describe a moment that is absent of any noise. Sometimes this brings comfort, but many times there is a feeling of awkwardness or anxiety. In that sense, many avoid complete silence by speaking to themselves, speaking with someone, or listening to something.

Today there is a dead silence I want to address head on. It is a silence that is sad, grievous, and deeply concerning. It is a prevailing silence of the government and church regarding the prevention of disease. In other words, it is the silence regarding stewardship of our temple (our earth suits), which is the greatest of all of God's creation.

This scripture comes to mind:

> "Deliver those who are drawn toward death. And hold back those stumbling to the slaughter. If you say, 'Surely we did not know this,' does not He who weighs the hearts consider it? He who keeps your soul, does He not know it? And will He not render to each man according to his deeds?" (Proverbs 24:11-12)

Or, as The Message version relates it: "Rescue the perishing; don't hesitate to step in and help. If you say, 'Hey, that's none of my business,' will that get you off the hook? Someone is watching you closely, you know—Someone not impressed with weak excuses."

What is this saying? It is saying that if, as disciples of Jesus Christ, we see others being led down paths of destruction and death (i.e. the potential shortening of life and therefore diminishing of God's ultimate purpose for each of us), we should say or do something. We cannot say in good conscience that it is none of our business. As disciples, our level of care for our fellow human needs to increase.

The church as a whole, as well as government, rarely mention anything about what our lifestyle is doing to our physical health. We hear a lot about deadly viruses, hospitalizations, sickness, fear of death, loss of jobs, elections, and economic turmoil. But what about some conversation on how to avoid needless disease processes? Why aren't there more leaders proclaiming wisdom about how to live well, the dangers of medication dependence, and healthy lifestyle protocols? This should be taught and broadcast from the mountaintops by every government official and every church leader (and every disciple of Jesus Christ for that matter). By not boldly proclaiming these truths, more people are being "drawn toward death" and "stumbling to the slaughter."

Friends, now is the time to wake up from our slumber, see through the darkness, arise out of our deceptions, and begin to speak about being good caretakers of our temples.

So many people are dying too early because of the dead silence.

53
Simple Instructions for Life

DR. MICHELE

Thinking and planning the New Year agenda brings me to the question of the 12th Verse of Psalm 34.

"Does anyone want to live a life that is long and prosperous?"

My hand is in the air, raised high with enthusiasm. I'm listening! The following verse is one prerequisite:

"Then keep your tongue from speaking evil and your lips from telling lies."

That is a hefty command as the tongue can be unbridled and chatter away with evil. We point fingers, blame, boast, tell untruths, all of which are forms of evil. But there's hope in verse 14.

"Turn away from evil and do good. Search for peace, and work to maintain it."

Searching for peace is a goal we should all have and diligently work to maintain. It is not easy sometimes in this broken world. We need more love and less hate. We need more laughter and less angst. And our actions are up to us! More truth and love in verse 15:

"The eyes of the Lord watch over those who do right, his ears are open to their cries for help."

That's right, He hears our cry for help. He steps into action to help all of his children, and He keeps his promises.

With all of these things (a bridled tongue, seeking peace, abandoning evil) done to the glory of God, He sees and adds health and prosperity.

Let's consider how we can follow these simple, beautiful instructions from Psalm 34 today.

54
Hope Dealers

DR. MICHELE

LET'S TURN TO THE BIBLE FOR EVERY DECISION, AT ALL TIMES, NOT JUST times of trouble. The instructions and wisdom we find there lead the way to life. If we follow them, we cannot fail, and we will please our Father in heaven. Pleasing people is a dead end street. God does not fail us, man does.

Questions are flying around these days as the world seems hopeless. Why?

A scripture comes to mind:

> *"Those who forget God have no hope. They are like rushes without any mire to grow in; or grass without water to keep it alive. Suddenly it begins to wither, even before it is cut. A man without God is trusting in a spider's web. Everything he counts on will collapse. If he counts on his home for security, it won't last."* (JOB 8:13-15 TLB)

Wow! We often get focused on the wrong things. We set our minds on earthly things that are all perishable. Instead, we need to focus on Jesus. He is the true "hope dealer" for all eternity.

Here is a scripture to focus on to provide hope!

> *"May the God of hope fill you with all joy and peace as you trust in him, so that you may overflow with hope by the power of the Holy Spirit."*
> *Romans 13:15)*

Being a hope dealer means helping people heal from sickness and disease, and also working to bring their minds and hearts back to our Father in heaven who is the real source of hope. He will fill us with joy and peace as we trust Him. Let go of fear; it is False Evidence Appearing Real. Fear will destroy your very being and create division in your life. The most tragic division is disconnection from our wonderful Creator.

Obtain your hope from the right source. The power source from above.

55

Men, Where are You?

DR. MARK

WHAT DOES IT MEAN TO BE A MAN? I HAVE ASKED MYSELF THAT QUESTION many times over my life. Without fail, I find there is no single answer but several.

Being a man is more than just having the anatomical structure of one. To get to the answer, let's go back in time, to the genesis of man.

If God created man in his own image, and if we hold the belief that God is good, then man must have been assigned, at least originally, with every characteristic of "good."

Before we explore these characteristics, let me state the obvious; I am not perfect. However, these facets of God's nature are worth striving for, every day. As the saying goes, "practice makes perfect" so let's practice these characteristics as perfectly as possible!

True manhood is defined in love.

This love is a sacrificial and exemplary love. It is a love that covers over all deficiencies and is, in itself, unexplainable. Practically speaking, it is a love for mankind, even though mankind is not perfect.

A real man will not love his life so much that he will not give it up for those he loves. This kind of love leads silently as an observed trait. It does not ask, it gives.

Manhood has the desire to provide for others.

Real men provide for their families, children, and other causes they deem beneficial for others. This is why men go off to war to fight for something in which they believe. It is why men go to work daily, even though sickness or fatigue may be a temporary part of their lives. This mentality of provision never stops deepening and growing in the heart of a true man.

Manhood is permeated by sacrifice.

A true man will go without so his family can have plenty. He will take the least, so that his family can have the most. He will give up his coat, and find himself cold, so that his wife can be warm. Real men cannot waiver in this sacrificial mentality as it is ingrained deeply in their core being.

Manhood is characterized by unwavering leadership.

A real man is the leader of his family: emotionally, spiritually, and physically. Simply put, he is calm and reassuring under pressure, he is solid in his faith, he eats well, exercises, and gets enough sleep. There is zero compromise in these foundational principles.

Manhood understands the power words.

Real men know that words matter, specifically the words "yes" and "no." Therefore, real men understand the obligation of agreement as well as the gravity of a decision. They do not waiver and are not blown about by changing emotions. When a man makes a decision, he does not do it rashly or abruptly, he does it with much thought and prayer, since the decision puts a permanent mark on his word.

So I ask myself, and all of you, the following questions:

1. Do I really exemplify *love* even when others do not?
2. Have I maintained and lived out a *provider* mentality?
3. Do I willingly *sacrifice*, or do I do it grudgingly?
4. Do I exhibit unwavering and predictable *leadership*?
5. Does my *word* mean something, and do I honor it?

These questions must be answered honestly if we, as men, desire to be a real man. Are the characteristics of true manhood challenging to live out? You bet they are! However, in a world where this type of manhood is becoming rare, the pursuit is worth it.

If men will simply stand up and become real men, admitting their many imperfections and flaws, and never wavering from their *pursuit* of true manhood, the world, and our communities will be a better place.

So, here's to manhood. Men, let's embrace these characteristics and truly begin the change this world needs.

By the way, if you're a woman, you have my permission to show this to the men in your life. But please don't "beat them over the head" with these words. Pray for them, encourage them, and love them as they grow through the process of manhood. And if you're unmarried, these characteristics would be a great start as a checklist for the spouse you deserve.

56
Leaning on God's Word

DR. MICHELE

Days can be doozies. Times can be troubled and intense. We have learned to expect the unexpected. Sometimes the unexpected lends the greatest opportunity for growth in all areas, physically, mentally, emotionally, and especially spiritually!

A scripture comes to mind :

"The Lord hears his people when they call to him for help. He rescues them from all their troubles. The Lord is close to the brokenhearted; he rescues those whose spirits are crushed." (PSALM 34: 17-18)

If you are having troubles in your life, pray without ceasing. Look to our Heavenly Father for help. We know that in this world we will have troubles, In this world we will have pain. We will also have joy, love, and blessing. If your spirit, soul, and body are weary, lean in to God's Word instead of your own limited understanding.

Here are some nuggets of Truth from the Bible.

I am a new creation in God. (2 CORINTHIANS 5:17)

I can walk by the Spirit. (GALATIANS 5:16-17)

I will be a light to all for my God. (MATTHEW 5:14)

I am content with the Lord. (PHILIPPIANS 4:11)

I am secure in the Lord. (ROMANS 8:38-39)

I am free in You, Lord. (ROMANS 6:18)

I am a child of God. (JOHN 1:12)

I am protected by God's angels. (PSALM 91:14-16)

The Lord is my refuge. (PSALM 91:9-10"

Enjoy some time right now, and throughout today, speaking these truths out loud.

57
Ten Signposts for the Narrow Road

DR. MICHELE

Mark and I have been reflecting on issues that seem to spin God's people out of control. Instantly my mind began to resonate on the following scriptures from Exodus 20. (These passages are where the narrow road splits from the wide road.)

> *"I am the Lord your God, who brought you out of Egypt, out of the land of slavery.*
>
> *"You shall have no other gods before me.*
>
> *You shall not make for yourself an image in the form of anything in heaven above or on the earth beneath or in the waters below.*
>
> *You shall not bow down to them or worship them; for I, the Lord your God, am a jealous God, punishing the children for the sin of the parents to the third and fourth generation of those who hate me, but showing love to a thousand generations of those who love me and keep my commandments.*
>
> *You shall not misuse the name of the Lord your God, for the Lord will not hold anyone guiltless who misuses his name.*
>
> *Remember the Sabbath day by keeping it holy. Six days you shall labor and do all your work, but the seventh day is a sabbath to the Lord your God. On it you shall not do any work, neither you, nor your son or daughter, nor your male or female servant, nor your animals, nor any*

foreigner residing in your towns. For in six days the Lord made the heavens and the earth, the sea, and all that is in them, but he rested on the seventh day. Therefore the Lord blessed the Sabbath day and made it holy.

Honor your father and your mother, so that you may live long in the land the Lord your God is giving you.

You shall not murder.

You shall not commit adultery.

You shall not steal.

You shall not give false testimony against your neighbor.

You shall not covet your neighbor's house. You shall not covet your neighbor's wife, or his male or female servant, his ox or donkey, or anything that belongs to your neighbor."

Wow. Can you see why the world is upside-down today?

We are not being salt and light, or sharpening each other, when we normalize immorality.

Perhaps it is time to repent. We the people must turn from our wicked ways as the following scripture reveals clearly.

> *"If my people, who are called by my name, will humble themselves and pray and seek my face and turn from their wicked ways, then I will hear from heaven, and I will forgive their sin and will heal their land."*
> (2 CHRONICLES 7:14)

Our Father in heaven is waiting. He is waiting for us to turn from our wicked ways, and he will heal our land.

Let's stand for God's Word today and allow Him to work through our lives.

58

A Fearful Epidemic (Part 1)

DR. MARK

We all watched as the world was gripped with fear over the COVID 19 virus. And even now, because of the perpetual bombardment of the news media, it is virtually impossible to escape the negative and debilitative effects of fear as it relates to human physiology.

Without question, chronic fear is destructive. So let's begin with a question to reflect on. "Do I perpetually speak about, read about, and dwell upon fear?"

Let's define fear. Generally, it is defined as: "A distressing emotion aroused by impending danger, evil, pain, etc., whether the threat is real or imagined; the feeling or condition of being afraid."

Fear leads to biological changes induced by adrenaline surges in the bloodstream. Adrenaline prepares the body for a *fight* or a *flight*. If, by chance, movement of blood from the cortex is too fast, one can even find themselves feeling faint, speechless, frozen in place. When fear occurs in our life, respiration, blood pressure, perspiration, and heart rate all increase. Our body is ready for an all-out attack, or a run for our life.

Biological changes can result from real or perceived threats. The majority of our negative issues result from perceived or imagined fear where we feel we do not have control over the outcomes. Think about it like this: *Can I really avoid the coronavirus? Can I avoid viruses at all? Should I live my life worrying about getting sick or not?*

Please understand, to live life is chronic fear is to *not* live life.

As we mentioned earlier, fear can sometimes be explained as the acronym: False Evidence Appearing Real.

Whether real or not, when fear strikes us, it is very real to us and impacts our mind and body in very real ways. Much of the fear today is strictly in the realm of imagination. It stems from past hurts, trauma, disappointments, and uncertainty. If we do not deal with fear in the proper way, the associated bodily responses become the norm.

Fear can be perpetually self-generated with questions such as: *What if I can't make enough money? What if this diet plan doesn't work? What if I get cancer? What if I don't make it? What if they don't like me?*

You will notice in each of these questions the two words, "what if." The answer is clearly unknown. However, when we allow these questions to dwell at the forefront of our thoughts, the emotion of fear will show its ugly head with a chronically-elevated bodily response. In this scenario, the emotions, questions, traumas, and dramas of fear become permanently ingrained in the computer-like database of our inner brain.

The good news is that we can choose another path for our thoughts. And we can abide in relationship with our God, who gives peace.

59
A Special Word from God to You

DR. MICHELE

I am speaking in the depths of your being. Be still so that you can hear My voice.

I speak in the language of love. My words fill you with Life and Peace, Joy and Hope.

I desire to talk with all of My children, but many are too busy to listen. The modern "work ethic" has them tied up in knots. They submit wholeheartedly to this taskmaster, wondering why they feel so distant from Me.

Living close to Me requires making Me your First Love, your highest priority. As you seek My Presence above all else, you experience peace and joy in full measure. I also am blessed when you make Me first in your life.

"The earth is filled with your love, O Lord; teach me your decrees."
(Psalm 119:64)

"The Sovereign Lord has given me an instructed tongue, to know the word that sustains the weary. He wakens me morning by morning, wakens my ear to listen like one being taught." (Isaiah 50:4)

"Yet I hold this against you: You have forsaken your first love."
(Revelation 2:4)

"See, darkness covers the earth and thick darkness is over the peoples, but the Lord rises upon you and his glory appears over you." (Isaiah 60:2)

While you journey through life in My Presence, My Glory brightens the world around you.

60
The Jezebel Spirit

DR. MICHELE

As we continue to fight the battle of maintaining our freedoms today we have to recognize the Jezebel spirit that is in political power, and vote it out. Scripture tells us of the nature of this spirit is as follows

> "Nevertheless, I have this against you: You tolerate that woman Jezebel, who calls herself a prophet. By her teaching she misleads my servants into sexual immorality and the eating of food sacrificed to idols." (Revelation 2:20)

Let's evaluate other signs of the Jezebel personality.

The Jezebel spirit is sociopathic (lack of empathy and disregards the rights of others). It has a huge ego and wants to meet its desire and need for power. The Jezebel spirit does this by assuming false authority by any means possible. With this false authority, the Jezebel spirit not only fulfills its need for power, but also gets tremendous ego satisfaction as it continually maneuvers for a position of control. Do you recognize this spirit in what is happening today?

1. They gain power by destroying others. It is like an adrenalin rush when they "win" over someone. They manage to get in positions of authority, and are difficult to displace, once there.
2. They are controlling, manipulative, bossy.
3. They can either be war-like in their personalities, so that they are intimidating, or so "sweet," "perfect," deceitful, "timid" and sneaky. They are able to fool and recruit others to join them. Sometimes they can be very charming and charismatic.

4. They are critical of others, vicious to the point of being bloodthirsty.
5. They never admit being wrong, even in the face of evidence.
6. They recruit others in their charges against their victims. They act to persuade recruits, and do not give up this activity until the recruits are won over. If the potential recruits do not cooperate and buy into things, this angers them. (Sounds familiar?)
7. They are narcissistic (self-important). While they can tend to be oversensitive themselves, they have no concern for the feelings of others. They are not sympathetic to their victims, and tend to play the role of victim themselves, in order to gain sympathy. This way the real victim is left stranded, and opposed by others if they ask for help. Being the center of attention really pleases them.
8. They falsely accuse you, and they do not forgive you.

These are just a few to beware of. We must become aware of what is going on in our world and we must obtain knowledge. First, let's make sure that these characteristics are not in our own spirit.

Scripture says, "My people perish from a lack of knowledge." (HOSEA 4:6 KJV)

We must educate ourselves on these intense topics. Let's be wise and evaluate every situation that appears to have the Jezebel spirit and work to get it removed from our lives, businesses, and our communities.

61
A Fearful Epidemic (Part 2)

DR. MARK

In my earlier reading, we discussed the devastatingly-negative physiological effects of chronic fear. We also defined both types of fear: real and imagined.

Let's explore the true roots of fear.

Chronic fear leads to elevated cortisol in our bodies. Elevated cortisol will lead to increased blood sugar, increased insulin production, dysfunctional sleep patterns, weight gain, dysfunctional metabolism, hormonal imbalance, and chronic inflammation.

We mistakenly try to correct each with pills, diet, and exercise. However, none of these truly address the root of the problem. To understand the root of the problem, allow me to quote one verse from the Bible.

> "For God did not give us a spirit of fear but of power, love, and of sound mind." (2 Timothy 1:7)

If God did not give us the spirit of fear, then who did? We know the answer to that question. A spirit of fear can barge its away into our thoughts. We realize how we feel, act, and respond to those around us when the spirit of fear consumes us. However, we underestimate the power of the spirit of fear in regard to the decay of our *health*.

So how do we overcome chronic fear? For the answer, I will again quote (in part) one passage from the Bible.

> "and so we know and rely on the love God has for us. God is love. Whoever lives in love lives in God, and God in him… There is no fear in love. But perfect love drives out fear…" (1 John 4:16-18)

So there you have it. God is the source of love, and He casts out all fear. It is not our job. Stop entertaining fear, speaking about fear, and fueling fear! Stop it now!

When we rely on God, who lives in us, it is his responsibility to make fear run the other way. You see, God makes fear run away. That's right, fear is mortally *afraid* in the presence of God's love. However, without God, fear can run rampant.

To trust God at His Word is to trust Him to get rid of the fear. When we are then filled with His love and peace, they exhibit themselves by lowering: blood pressure, respiration, heart rate, and perspiration. Chronic and debilitating health conditions, as mentioned above, are reduced. In turn, we find ourselves in a state of wellness and peace rather than the state of dis–ease.

If this reading resonates with you, share it boldly with others. Living in fear is death. Living free from chronic fear is abundant life. This life is God's true intent for us. As we live by the light of God's love, fear will run for the hills.

62

Cowardice or Courage

DR. MICHELE

BECAUSE I ALWAYS WANT TO EQUIP YOU FOR LIVE ON THE NARROW road, I share this recent experience. A "dreadful" thought came to mind after ministering to a patient who's heart was broken by a tragic rumor.

I encourage you to do *good* deeds for others, instead of using the tongue to spread rumors, negativity, and lies! Instead, go directly to your brother or sister and do good. Our greatest gift is service, and that does not mean *lip service*!

Let's consider the life of Moses. He didn't want to go back to Egypt as one to confront the Pharaoh. You can be sure that every time the Lord made the request, or gave the orders to do so, Moses "dreaded" it. "Send someone else" would be his reply. (EXODUS 4:13)

Perhaps that's why it's so hard to go to our brother or sister and confront wrongdoing or miscommunication. It's *dreadful* to imagine their negative reply. It's much easier to go to others, gossip, and be told that we're "right."

But, note that once Moses agreed to be God's agent in freeing his own flesh and blood from slavery (in our day today, free yourself from gossip and turn a deaf ear to those who do), much benefit resulted his people.

Step out of the trenches of wrongdoing! Put them behind you. Instead choose love and acts of service.

When we feel convinced we should do something that would benefit someone else, but then realize the cost involved, don't we hesitate?

We often struggle with dreadful, foreboding thoughts before taking the right action. Yet, when we find enough courage to go through with it, aren't we glad we did?

Before Jesus hung on the cruel cross of Calvary, and while in the Garden of Gethsemane, He cried out, "Father, let this cup pass from me!" I suppose we can say that as a human He dreaded the cruel manner of death that waited Him. Yet, He added, "Nevertheless, not My will, but Yours be done!"

What a daily reminder and prayer!

The Bible verse that brings this truth home to me like none other comes from Hebrews 12:2.

"Let us fix our eyes on Jesus, the author and perfecter of our faith, who for the joy that was set before Him, endured the cross, scorning its shame, and sat down at the right hand of the throne of God."

As God in human flesh, Jesus knew the outcome of His suffering and death. He realized the impact upon all humanity. Thus, "for the joy that was set before Him" he chose to obey The Father.

Remember, gossip is easy, but promotes cowardice. Straight talk in love is hard, but promotes courage.

63
A Spiritual Check-Up

DR. MICHELE

From time to time, it is good to do a spiritual check in, just like we go for medical check-ups. Just recently, I had an oil change and an annual check on various functions of my car. As I waited for the results, I began to ponder relationships, both human and divine.

How am I doing in my relationships with those around me, and with my Savior? We can get lost in the busyness of life and easily forget. Do I consider these relationships important enough for regular check-ups?

Scriptures come to mind:

"Examine yourselves to see whether you are living in the faith. Test yourselves. Do you not realize that Jesus Christ is in you, unless of course you've failed to meet the Test?" (2 Corinthians 13:5)

"Let each test his own work. Then, he will have rejoicing in himself alone and not in another." (Galatians 6:4)

How do I check out when I test myself and my lifestyle relative to: faith issues, family matters, friendships, and new interactions? Very often, I recognize some need of repair and the necessity of regular maintenance for a full and healthy life. We've all experienced the blessings of good relationships. Broken ones give us headaches and heartaches.

Investing in tune-ups pays off and leads to "rejoicing"! Who do you need to check in with today?

64
The Enemy of Healing

DR. MARK

When you consider humanity's ever-increasing struggles, and desire, for wellness, is there any doubt that we're in a battle? Shouldn't we be further along? Just look at the upward trend in the use of pharmaceutical medications. Dr. Michele and I are not against pharmaceutical drugs, but we are very passionately against the overuse and unnecessary use of medications.

Why? Because medications are not about healing disease. Medications are about *managing* conditions.

If we believe that God is all about healing, then we can't believe God is completely satisfied by the mere management of sickness and disease. Let's look at Galatians 5:19–20:

> *"Now the works of the flesh are evident: sexual immorality, impurity, sensuality, idolatry, sorcery, enmity, strife, jealousy, fits of anger, rivalries, dissensions, divisions."*

The Apostle Paul, under God's direction, is talking to the Galatian church about the decline of their lifestyle. Regarding the word "sorcery," the original Greek word is *pharmakeia*, from which we derive the words *pharmacy* and *pharmaceutical*.

There seems to be a view of pharmakeia and sorcery working hand in hand, indicating that a dependence upon drugs to bring about healing is a form of substitution or distraction from the real source of health.

Even in the most recent pandemic, we are still searching and looking for a "pill for the ill." Isn't there something deeply troubling about that?

A sole dependence upon drugs to heal certainly doesn't agree with the biblical principle.

What about insurance? There seems to be no escaping many forms of insurance in our society. Homeowners, auto, health, and endless other forms of coverage.

The question to consider is this: *When does insurance pay?*

The answer is: *When something goes wrong.*

When does car insurance pay? When the car breaks. Does car insurance pay for oil changes, tune-ups, or fuel? *No.*

When does health insurance pay? *When you're sick.*

"Health insurance" is probably an improper term. Really, it's sick insurance.

Insurance is important, but too many people have been lulled into dependence on pharmaceutical and insurance companies. (And in our view, more money is spent on the advertising a medication—to fuel this dependence—than is invested in the research and development of the product.)

Insurance is a for-profit business, and consistent customers are the best source of consistent income for this industry. We need to understand how to keep that money in our pockets. That's what "well care" does—it keeps the deductible in your pocket. Every year.

The best way to get well is to ask God to grant a new perspective and mindset. He does not need drugs and insurance to produce healing in our lives.

65
A Model of Good

DR. MICHELE

The phrase "What you see is what you get" was often used to describe retail showroom "models." Sometimes the buyers wouldn't get what they paid for, which created not only disappointment, but anger and resentment.

This makes me reflect on my life as a Christian. How do we define a "model" Christian, and when defined, does our life come close? Do people who know us get anything close to expectations? A scripture or two come to mind.

> *"Show yourself in all respects a model of good works."* (Titus 2:7)

Okay, but what does a model of good works look like? From Titus 3:1, the model begins to take shape: "Be ready for every good work."

A readiness or willingness to become a model is essential! Alright, but then what? From the letter to Titus again: "Those who who come to believe in God may be careful to devote themselves to good works... things that are excellent and profitable." (Titus 3:8)

We must be really committed to the worthwhile stuff of living! What's that? Back to scripture.

> *"The grace of God has appeared, bringing salvation to all, training us to renounce impiety and worldly passions, and in this present age to live lives that are self-controlled, upright, and godly."* (Titus 2:11)

Self-controlled, upright, and godly: that model looks a lot like Jesus!

What is the Holy Spirit showing you about how to better model Jesus in this world?

66
Life and Peace

DR. MICHELE

LIFE IS JOYFUL, LIFE IS CURIOUS, AND LIFE CAN BE CHALLENGING WITH each passing year (or sometimes with each passing moment).

Challenges are… challenging. In fact they can be gut wrenching at times. Jesus tells us that even in darkness, *be the light.*

A Scripture comes to mind:

"While I am in the world, I am the light of the world." (JOHN 9:5)

Just as Jesus is, we are to be a light that shines in the darkness. Light, no matter how dim, still illuminates dark roads and treacherous paths.

No matter what comes across your path, fear not. Fear is deadly. Fear dries up the bones and is death to the soul. Fear causes division and indecisiveness. Fear is ruthless on our physical and mental health.

Scripture states:

"So do not fear, for I am with you; do not be dismayed, for I am your God. I will strengthen you and help you; I will uphold you with my righteous right hand." (ISAIAH 41:10)

God's promises are real. When struggle ensues, recall yet another scripture:

"Peace I leave with you; my peace I give you. I do not give to you as the world gives. Do not let your hearts be troubled and do not be afraid." (JOHN 14:27)

With peace, and in the absence of fear, our light will shine brighter.

Pursue peace. Aim to be a bright light in this dark world. Eradicate all evidence of fear in our lives, and shine with peace from within today!

67
Living with a Winning Mindset

DR. MARK

WHAT DOES IT REALLY MEAN TO HAVE A WINNING MINDSET? It is much more than we realize. The Bible speaks clearly of renewing the mind.

> "Do not conform to the pattern of this world, but be transformed by the renewing of your mind. Then you will be able to test and approve what God's will is—his good, pleasing and perfect will." (ROMANS 12:2)

Think for a moment about the words: *do not conform, be transformed,* and *renew*. They paint a great picture of being different by thinking differently, which brings a transformative difference.

To that end, here is some encouragement to truly have the winning and transformative mindset:

1. Thinking Big vs Thinking Small
Those with an abundant mindset are renowned for thinking big, it is part of their DNA. Scarcity mindset creates limitations in the mind which prevents the creation of audacious goals.

2. Plenty vs Lack
Those with an abundant mentality believe there is plenty of everything in the world, from resources, love, relationships, wealth, and opportunities. They believe they can afford what they want in life and say what they believe: "I can afford that!"

Those with a lack mentality prefer to believe that there are limited opportunities, resources, relationships, love, wealth, and opportunities.

They consistently say: "I will never afford that." Speaking statements of lack reinforces the belief, and forms that exact pattern in reality.

3. Happiness vs Resentment
Someone with an abundant mentality is an optimist and is genuinely happy for others when they achieve success. Conversely, those with a scarcity mindset are competitive and resent other's success.

4. Embracing Change vs Fear of Change
A person with an abundant mindset understands that change is an integral part of life, They embrace and accept change. Appreciating the fact that change often leads to more positive outcomes, even if change is somewhat challenging to navigate.

Fear plagues those with a scarcity mindset. They will spend time constantly complaining along about change and take a longer period of time to accept change.

5. Proactive vs Reactive
Due to the positive attitude of those with a winning mindset, they take a proactive approach to life. Rather than waiting for things to happen and then reacting, like those with a scarcity mindset do, they strategically plan for a bright future.

6. Learning vs Knowing It All
An abundance mentality craves learning and growth. They have a never-ending thirst for knowledge and developing new skills. But a scarcity mindset believes they know everything, thereby severely limiting their learning and growth.

7. What Is Working vs What Is Not Working
A person with a scarcity mindset selects negative thoughts and adopts a victim mentality.

The strong emotions they experience create stress in the body with the range of feelings shifting from anxiety, fear, worry, anger and resentment.

Their negative emotions, thoughts, and beliefs create illnesses in the body, leading to generally poor health. Their daily focus is on what is *not* working.

Those with a winning mindset are often visionaries and see the limitless possibilities in the world. Their focus in daily life is on what *is* working.

The path forward is not set in stone. Such is the beauty of life; you can change. Deciding to change paths is the first step. Life is short. Live large. Believe in the endless possibilities life has to offer and choose to live an abundant life!

68
Technical Support

DR. MICHELE

Yesterday on my computer, a certain e-mail program just didn't work, no matter what I tried. When something like this happens, I call a friend for tech help. He always seems to solve the problem.

After everything was working smoothly again, the thought came about our Friend, Jesus. We can call on Him anytime, anywhere, and for whatever reason. This scripture comes to mind from John 15:15. To His disciples, Jesus said, "I have called you friends."

Reminds me of that familiar Hymn, "What a Friend we have in Jesus." How amazing, Jesus chooses to be our Friend! Take a moment to ponder this mind-blowing truth.

Whatever life "program" we face, Jesus, our Friend, is on call 24/7. Calling Him, we never get a busy signal, and we are never put on hold. And God never changes his plans on us!

What issues do you need help with today? Call on our Friend, Jesus, Who assists us with all of life's programs. All things are possible with Him.

69
Hold On!

DR. MICHELE

WE RESOLVE TO GROW SPIRITUALLY, STAY STRONG PHYSICALLY AND well-balanced emotionally. Will you say this out loud, and improve your day?

I resolve to grow spiritually, stay strong physically, and well-balanced emotionally.

Scripture comes to mind. "Keep your eyes open, hold on tight to your convictions, give it all you have got, be resolute." (1 CORINTHIANS 16:13)

It is easy to get pulled off course and find yourself back in the ditch and participating in old habits, or choices that are destructive to you and your family. Stand resolved!

Scripture also says, "In this world you will have trouble. Take heart I have overcome the world." (JOHN 16:13)

Hold on tight to your convictions! Be resolved. Speak them boldly and triumphantly. If the wind blows you in a drafty direction, look to the Word and you will find stability, and instructions for getting you through the storm.

And when the sun shines, God's Word will bring gratitude, humility, and power.

70

Too Much of a Good Thing?

DR. MARK

Can one exercise too much? The short answer is yes! A pattern of chronic exercise in pursuit of extreme or narrowly-focused fitness goals can trigger increased cravings for quick energy carbohydrates, inhibit fat metabolism, compromise immune function, exhaust the body's stress-management mechanisms, and break down lean muscle tissue.

Yes, you read that correctly, too much exercise can indeed *break down* muscle tissue. It is unfortunate that many believe they must exercise more to get better results. However, it is important to understand how to exercise patiently without becoming chronic.

"There is a time for everything, and a season for every activity under the heavens" (ECCLESIASTES 3:1)

Chronic exercise stimulates hormonal changes in the body that actually promote fat storage. We have seen this many times in our practice regarding persons who are doing chronically, intense workout sessions five or more times per week. There is simply not enough rest to recover. This often results in the retention of ten pounds or more excess weight from fat storage.

It should be noted that a chronic cardio exercise pattern has also been shown to obstruct immune system function, destroy white blood cells, elevate cortisol levels, suppress testosterone levels, and trigger systemic inflammation. As you might infer, adding testosterone therapy to a self-imposed dysfunctional system will not provide the desired results. Testosterone is an adaptive, muscle building, mood elevating, cognitive performance enhancing, anti-aging hormone for both males and females, while cortisol is the primary catabolic stress hormone. These two hormones antagonize each other, so chronically elevated cortisol will suppress testosterone.

We advise doing the following in regard to exercise:
1. Maintain an active lifestyle. Avoid becoming sedentary at all costs. This means making a point to stand more at work, walk more, and simply move more as a pattern of everyday life.
2. Conduct very infrequent sessions of high-intensity training throughout the week. Exercise different muscle groups on different days. They can total two or three, and sometimes four, sessions per week.
3. Conduct regular sessions of steady aerobic type of training. This may consist of treadmill, walking, jogging, elliptical, or rowing machine.

Never, and I mean never, use exercise as the main mechanism in regard to managing your weight. Your greatest return investment will come from balanced nutritional practices, effective stress management, and sufficient sleep.

Put this knowledge into practice immediately. Your body will love it, and the results will show themselves over a lifetime.

71
Trust God and Do Good

DR. MICHELE

Challenging times these days. Seems people are *hurting* each other more than *hello-ing* each other. Hate fills the air and crushes peace. Once again, Psalm 34: 12-16 comes to mind.

> "Does anyone want to live a life that is long and prosperous?
> Then keep your tongue from speaking evil and your lips from telling lies.
> Turn away from evil and do good.
> Search for peace, and work to maintain it.
> The eyes of the Lord watch over those who do right; his ears are open to their cries for help.
> But the Lord turns his face against those who do evil."

I would not want the Lord to turn his face against me. What a painful day that would be. With the challenges we have faced he has never left our side.

In all our days, and especially today, let us continue to dig deep, give when we are tired, nurture when we need to be nurtured, and express love to souls who are lost to turn their hearts towards Jesus.

Let's overcome evil with good.

Our cries for help will always be primarily to God, and not "man." Yes we need each other, however we know people will fail us, and sometimes let us down us when we need help the most!

Bring goodness to your neighbors today, and bring your requests to God.

72
Faith Over Fear

DR. MICHELE

The word of the day is faith over fear. Fear destroys our health and relationships. It is time to grow our faith and abolish fear.

Scripture comes to mind.

> *"Later Jesus appeared to the Eleven as they were eating; he rebuked them for their lack of faith and their stubborn refusal to believe those who had seen him after he had risen. He said to them, "Go into all the world and preach the gospel to all creation. Whoever believes and is baptized will be saved, but whoever does not believe will be condemned. And these signs will accompany those who believe: In my name they will drive out demons; they will speak in new tongues; they will pick up snakes with their hands; and when they drink deadly poison, it will not hurt them at all; they will place their hands on sick people, and they will get well."* (Mark 16:14)

Jesus was not afraid to lay hands on the sick, He has relentless faith. He creates unity with His actions and not division. His capability to teach the gospel transforms lives and deals hope! Division is busted to dust.

We need to be more like Jesus. Let's go into all the world, preach the gospel to all nations, pray for the sick, cast out demons, and lead others away from destruction. We must believe again and not live our lives in fear.

73

Death by Disorganization

DR. MARK

Disorganization is rampant in our society. It rears its ugly head through anger, chaos, emotional instability, and the feeling of being overwhelmed. Symptoms include depression, fatigue, financial debt, and even weight gain. Many of these symptoms can be avoided by simply instituting a few basic principles.

But first, one must face head-on the answer to the question, "Are you an organized person?"

To determine an answer, please consider the following questions:
1. Are you normally late to appointments?
2. Do you pick up your clothes from the floor?
3. Do you return phone calls, emails, and text messages in a timely manner (normally within 24 hours)?
4. Do you pick up your trash?
5. Do you maintain a healthy and consistent exercise program?
6. Do you eat fast food three or more times weekly?
7. Do you routinely get 7-9 hours of sleep?
8. Do you keep a to-do list or schedule of events?
9. Do your dishes pile up in the sink?
10. Do you complete routine physical, dental, or visual examinations?
11. Are you forgetful?
12. Are you routinely stressed (anxiety, fear, irritability)?
13. Do you routinely feel as if you have lost control?
14. Do you believe you are without hope?
15. Is your car clean (inside and out)?
16. Are you normally fatigued with a reliance on caffeine or sugar to keep you going?

17. Have you been in a pattern of weight gain from excess fat?
18. Are you forgetful?

If you answered YES to five or more questions, you are likely in a state of chronic disorganization. (And if you didn't catch an item repeated in the list above, that's a clear sign of forgetfulness!) If disorganization is not dealt with, one can experience a debilitating cascade of events.

For example, being routinely late can promote stress which leads to imbalances in the normal responses to life. This in turn creates an overabundance of stress hormones (adrenaline and cortisol). The overabundance of the freeze, fight, or flight hormones leads to dysfunction in the endocrine system, creates systemic inflammation, and leads to a pattern of excess fat gain. As we know, inflammation is a precursor for all sickness and disease. A pattern of being late hurts relationships, both personal and professional, which adds stress.

If life has become like this, there is good news. Here are some ways:
1. Work on arriving at appointments fifteen minutes early.
2. Purpose to sit in silence at least ten minutes a day. Turn off all distractions. Start at one minute if ten seems impossible.
3. Always have a to-do notebook and schedule handy. Write down important things to accomplish, people to call, and places to be. Cross them off the list when complete, and enjoy the accomplishment.
4. Pay all bills on time and do not live on credit. Selling things and downsizing may be in order.
5. Declutter your closet by giving away clothes and shoes. If you haven't worn it in two years, donate it.
6. Work on improving sleep by practicing good sleep hygiene (pre-bed routine, soothing baths, cool and dark room, no caffeine or sugar at least five hours prior to planned bed time).
7. Practice prayer and meditation on scripture. Dr. Michele and I reach out to God and ask for help.
8. Get a routine physical exam. Most insurance carriers allow one annually without cost.

9. Schedule at least three walks per week. Work on time and distance later. Enjoy yourself.
10. Make a conscious effort to smile and laugh more. There is far too much pain in the world. Make your environment happy.
11. Read an inspirational book or blog and purpose to spend time with positive people who lift your spirits.
12. Schedule a day to clean your house and car. The cleanliness will lead to satisfaction and joy in your soul.
13. Learn to forgive yourself. If you fall down, keep getting up. Do not stay down and feel sorry for yourself.

To move from disorganization and chaos to organization and order takes is a journey. I like to say it is a *Quest for Wellness*.

74
Watchful and Discerning

DR. MICHELE

We know where the Truth comes from., but are we watchful about how many lies we are bombarded with every day?

It's important to evaluate how many places can be sources of deception: television, social media, newspapers, and people who are not speaking or living in truth. We must have a discerning mind and thought process in order to keep these lies off of our lives.

We become what we spend our time with. The cunning ways of darkness are sneaky. Can you discern those sneaky ways?

This scripture comes to mind.

> "You are of your father the devil, and the desires of your father you want to do. He was a murderer from the beginning, and does not stand in the truth, because there is no truth in him. When he speaks a lie, he speaks from his own resources, for he is a liar and the father of it." (JOHN 8:44)

The prince of destruction comes to kill steal and destroy. (JOHN 10:10) He's full of nothing but lies—lying is his native tongue.

I remember a song from childhood:
O be careful little eyes what you see
O be careful little eyes what you see
There's a Father up above
And He's looking down in love
So, be careful little eyes what you see
O be careful little ears what you hear
O be careful little ears what you hear
There's a Father up above

And He's looking down in love
So, be careful little ears what you hear
O be careful little hands what you do
O be careful little hands what you do
There's a Father up above
And He's looking down in love
So, be careful little hands what you do
O be careful little feet where you go
O be careful little feet where you go
There's a Father up above
And He's looking down in love
So, be careful little feet where you go
O be careful little mouth what you say
O be careful little mouth what you say
There's a Father up above
And He's looking down in love
So, be careful little mouth what you say!

This resonates as our father is looking down in love letting us know to be on the lookout for all the ways we can wander off the narrow road.
Take time to pause and practice spiritual discernment today.

_____

_____

_____

_____

_____

# 75

Liberty for the Oppressed

DR. MARK

Church, what are we doing with our health?

I ask this question with a sincere heart. We are at an all-time high in our country in chronic sickness and disease. Heart disease is the number-one killer. Cancer is a close second. Type 2 diabetes affects one in three persons today. Obesity is the fastest growing non-communicable disease in the history of the world.

Has healing gone by the wayside?

With a broken heart, my wife and I weep many tears over the brokenness of mankind. We grieve over the money, time, and stress people pour out because of needless issues. *Needless* you say? Yes! The majority of the above-described diseases, and subsequent trends, are caused by our own behaviors. These behaviors manifest into disease processes.

As a matter of fact, the majority of the physical manifestations of disease we face today in America are rooted in physical or emotional brokenness.

In Luke 4:18-19 we read, "The Spirit of the LORD is upon Me, Because He has anointed Me To preach the gospel to the poor; He has sent Me to heal the brokenhearted, to proclaim liberty to the captives and recovery of sight to the blind, to set at liberty those who are oppressed; to proclaim the acceptable year of the LORD."

Maybe the real issue today is we have not really allowed our Lord to heal our hearts, take us out of self-imposed bondage, and give us sight to really see.

Proverbs 27:6 states, "Faithful are the wounds from a friend, but the kisses of an enemy are deceitful."

Allow me to be a friend who will show love with a difficult statement. Our society, and even the church, is short-circuiting our lives one fork at a time. We are consuming the standard American diet and using it even as a bait to draw people to gatherings. This is not of God or from God. This is strictly a cultural norm that has infiltrated spiritual leaders and brought about an influence that has manifested with debilitating, distracting, and costly diseases on the people of God. It is literally crushing our witness to the world.

I could go on, but this is enough for now. With a broken heart, I write these words to you all. Please receive them with the heart of love my wife and I have for you.

76

He Can Handle It

DR. MICHELE

All humans are tempted to worry. I'm not talking about "concern" which brings needed focus and leads to positive action. But why worry?

Worry builds a massive mound of despairing thoughts that rob the mind of healthy thinking and proper doing. Jesus had much to say about what we earthlings ought to ponder and practice for the best kind of living. Matthew 6:34 addresses the issue of worry in this way:

> *"Do not worry about tomorrow, for tomorrow will bring worries of its own. Today's trouble is enough for today."*

Will we be alive tomorrow? Who knows? Will tomorrow be filled with the bad or the good? Who can see the future? What good will worrying do?

Now, let's look back to yesterday, because we know something about that. Good things? Yes, a few. Tough issues? Yes, that too. We could worry about that also adding to the stress of this day. Then, we could add a bunch of tomorrow's worries. That would heap the worry pile mighty high, but will that make for a good day? Of course not!

I guess we really can't find a good reason to worry, can we? Yet, we all do it and suffer the consequences of it.

Well, then, what can we do about it? Jesus offers this advice, just preceding His words above:

> *"Seek first the kingdom of God and His righteousness and all these things will be yours as well."* (Matthew 6:33)

Earlier in His famous sermon, Jesus addressed the issues that cause us to worry, and gave His advice: When worries come, give them to God. He cares about whatever effects us, and can handle anything we give to Him.

To this, we can say, "Why not give my worries to God? He can handle it, and we can't!"

Mark and I have our worries, too, but we pray and do our best to quickly leave them with our loving God who cares enough, and can do what it takes, to handle them for us.

77
Picky Eaters

DR. MICHELE

Back in the day with grandma and grandpa on the farm (which seems like ages ago), I learned some things about animals, and more than just what they're good for. Horses help get various farm jobs done. Cows produce milk. Chickens lay eggs. You know, the basics.

But I also learned that these creatures can be quite discerning. For example, they sometimes turn away from certain types of food, like moldy hay.

Some harvests when it was rainy, it was extremely difficult to produce completely dry hay. Wet hay would mold and would be refused by horses and cows, even if it looked and smelled quite good to me.

Life for us is full of "moldy" stuff, which can have a negative effect on us. I believe you know where I'm going with this.

> *"Be careful, or your hearts will be weighed down with dissipation, drunkenness, and the anxieties of life... Be always on the watch and pray."* (Luke 21:34, 36)

Think about those who inspect fruits and vegetables while those products move along the conveyor table belt. Watchful eyes and quick hands pick out what's not good. We need to be just as watchful and quick to throw away the bad and keep the good. One more Scripture comes to mind.

> *"We must pay close attention, therefore, to what we have heard so that we don't drift away."* (Hebrews 2:1)

We have heard the good news from the scriptures. Abiding in God's Word gives us keen eyes to see both the good and bad, and to be skilled in making the right "picks."

Be "picky" with what you choose to think about today.

78
Honoring the Temple

DR. MARK

WE CLEARLY UNDERSTAND THE FOLLOWING TWO SCRIPTURES, OR do we?

> *"Don't you realize that all of you together are the temple of God and that the Spirit of God lives in you? God will destroy anyone who destroys this temple. For God's temple is holy, and you are that temple."* (1 CORINTHIANS 3:16-17)

> *"Don't you realize that your body is the temple of the Holy Spirit, who lives in you and was given to you by God? You do not belong to yourself, for God bought you with a high price. So you must honor God with your body."* (1 CORINTHIANS 6:19-20)

If we do understand, we would agree the following are true:
- The temple (our body) was purchased with the blood (sacrifice) of Jesus. Therefore, it is NOT our own.
- If we (or anyone else) destroy the temple, God will deal with them.
- Honoring (respecting and appreciating) your body is not a suggestion, but an order.

If these principles are true, then we must reconcile these obvious shortcomings in the culture of the church:
- We typically gather and fellowship with a focus on food, that being mostly "non-foods" that are damaging to the body.
- Youth groups and similar functions utilize these same non-foods as enticements to increase the size of gatherings.

As a reminder, the following foods in their natural state are good for us (let's call these anti-inflammatory foods):
- Quality proteins – organic, grass fed and finished, free range, wild caught
- Healthy oils and fats – olive oil, coconut oil, avocado, nuts, seeds
- Low glycemic fruits – berries, oranges, apples
- Low glycemic non-root, non-starchy vegetables

Please note that the following are considered non-foods (let's call these inflammatory foods):
- Sugars/artificial sweeteners
- Fried foods
- MSG and other "filler" chemicals
- Processed foods
- Sodas
- Breads and grains
- Yeast
- Soy
- Corn

In laying out the above, we are faced with several decisions:
- Do we continue to willingly abuse the temple and go against God's divine order?
- Do we repent and change our behavior?
- Do we make a conscious decision that my wife and I are simply wrong about what we wrote above?

Our temples are deteriorating more rapidly than God's intent, and that breaks my heart.

We are becoming society that is chronically inflamed, immunocompromised, and dependent on medications. This is not God's way.

What is your decision and what will you do? Change will take courage. Will you exhibit courage right now?

79
Clean and Clear

DR. MICHELE

We sometimes hear people refer to themselves as "old folks," and say things like, "At least I have my mind" as they chat about the challenges of old age.

What a precious, God-given gift, this mind of ours. But what about the conscience, which helps keep our minds sharp and focused on what's right and wrong? Indeed, our Creator also gave us the gift of a conscience.

Listen to the testimony of the Apostle Paul about his conscience and its effect on both divine and human relationships:

> "I do my best to have a clear conscience toward God and all people." (Acts 24:16)

We all know the misery of a guilty conscience whether in our relationship to God or people. Also, we know something about the sweetness of a clear conscience, which comes through making right choices and through the forgiveness experienced in Christ Jesus!

We can hide some of our misbehavior from other people, but never from the Lord. To deal with our foolish shortcomings (sins), our loving God provides His Word of truth which enlightens the conscience to decipher right from wrong. So, yet another passage from the Holy Book:

> "I am speaking the truth in Christ. I am not lying. My conscience confirms it by the Holy Spirit." (Romans 9:1)

The Spirit impresses and confirms God's claims and commands upon our consciences, and persuades us to trust Christ for all the clean-up and corrections necessary. What then should be our response as we live in a world where "anything goes"?

Of course, allow the Holy Spirit to do what God intended; reveal the sin and give grace to walk the narrow road. We receive this when we humbly and willingly seek the Lord in prayer, and also asking others for their prayers on our behalf, as this verse indicates:

> *"Pray for us, we are sure that we have a clear conscience, desiring to act honorably in all things."* (HEBREWS 13:18)

Yes, a clear conscience and acting honorably in all things. That's our pursuit today.

80
You've Got My Word on It

DR. MICHELE

In today's world of wheelings and dealings, we often hear the expression, "You've got my word on it." The New Testament writers included much material about the word. They referenced the prophetic Word often, and how it related to Jesus, who "became flesh and dwelt among us."

Jesus speaks about the importance of His own Word, and how that relates to the prophetic Word. Luke quotes Jesus as saying: "These are My words that I spoke to you while I was still with you that everything written about Me in the law of Moses, the prophets, and the Psalms must be fulfilled." (Luke 24:44-45)

Let's ponder on the truth of God saying: "You've got My Word on it."

The truth is that the Almighty not only gives us His Word, but He can fulfill it and make good on every promise!

Consider that, in a very real sense, Jesus Christ is The Promise kept, and think about what that means to you and your day today.

Consider also, the Bible stories of believers who bear witness to the truth that *God keeps His Word*.

God keeps His Word, even when others don't!

81
Overcoming with an Attitude

DR. MARK

As a child, I was frumpy, and sometimes chunky, a bit weak, and I was occasionally picked on. Believe it or not, once in a while when I look in the mirror, I see that chunky, frumpy kid.

Fast forward a few decades. After trying for a couple of years and failing to make a career in professional baseball, I became a police officer.

While working in the police department, I began to observe a very disturbing pattern. I watched how men and women would join the police department in the best shape of their lives and die in the worst shape of their lives shortly after retirement.

And they weren't living very long in age. 66 years on average. This shocked me, because I was on track to be one of the people who made this average expectancy so low.

I tell a bit of my story to let you know something important; I know what it's like to look in the mirror and not like what you see!

According to a recent poll, 61% of respondents said they gained weight during the pandemic. Most of those gained an average of 29 pounds. 10% of respondents gained over 50 pounds!

So why is being overweight such a problem for so many people? One reason is that we don't confront the problem honestly.

If I was your neighbor and saw that your house was on fire, I'd sound the alarm and make sure you were safe! Well, our bodies *are* our houses, and I'm here to tell you that if you're overweight, your house is on fire!

I needed a new attitude to make big lifestyle and career changes. You can have a new attitude, too.

I love the Bible story of Caleb. He was a go-getter. Even God took notice! After following God wholeheartedly into his eighties, he wanted more. Here are Caleb's own words:

"So here I am today, eighty-five years old! I am still as strong today as the day Moses sent me out (40 years ago). I'm just as vigorous to go out to battle now as I was then. Now give me this hill country that the Lord promised me that day." (Joshua 14)

You and I can adopt the same attitude. Changes take time (much less than forty years) but with the right attitude, better habits will form.

My research shows that your palate will even change in about two months, meaning foods you thought you couldn't live without will lose their appeal over time.

Ready to put on a new attitude today?

82

Paths of Peace

DR. MICHELE

Do you ever wonder if you are on the right path?
Do you wonder if your choices are the right ones?
Do you wonder if your life matters?
Consider this word from Jesus.

"Who of you by worrying can add a single hour to his life? Since you cannot do this very little thing, why do you worry about the rest?" (LUKE 12:25-26)

As we abide in God and His Word, we walk on a path of the Lord's choosing. The here and the now comprise the coordinates of your daily life. Most people let their moments slip though their fingers, half-lived. We often avoid the present by worrying about the future or longing for a better time and place.

The right path involves being in constant communion with our creator. With this constant relationship, you have no time for worry. You are free to let the Holy Spirit direct your steps, enabling you to walk along the path of peace.

"To shine on those living in darkness and in the shadow of death to guide our feet into the path of peace." (LUKE 1:79)

We must, of course, make good decisions for our life, strive for excellence, press in, and step up. If we continue to seek God as the center of our lives, we can maintain peace in the process.

Your life matters, every minute of it! Enjoy your peaceful path today.

83
A Radiant Reflection

DR. MICHELE

Have you ever thought about how much we communicate with just the look on our face?

There's the guilty look when a child gets caught with their hand in the cookie jar.

Imagine the delightfully surprised look, when a young maiden receives a ring and a marriage proposal.

We know the glazed expression, like when a person is very deep in thought.

When a student looks over their excellent report card or diploma, we often see a pleased look.

A worried look appears after being "hit" with bad news.

The radiant look expresses complete confidence, true wholeness, and genuine happiness. Such looks brings to mind this Scripture:

> "I sought the Lord and He answered me and delivered me from all my fears. Look to Him and be radiant; so your faces shall never be ashamed. This poor soul cried, and was heard by the Lord... O taste and see that the Lord is good. Happy are those who take refuge in Him." (Psalm 34:4-6, 8)

Focusing on the radiant look, and considering the above passage from the Psalms, let's take these simple steps:
1. *Desire* that radiant look. After all
2. who doesn't want to live with confidence, true wholeness, and genuine happiness, the kind that lasts even when the "going gets tough"?

3. *Trust* the Lord, Who provides this radiant look, when He transforms the inner character. After all, that's why Jesus came! He paid for the proper heart and "facial" for each of us.
4. *Take* the faith step necessary for that blessed, radiant look to reflect on you: "Look to Him and be radiant!"

Meditate on the above verses, direct your attention on God, and radiate His love today!

84
Turning Around

DR. MARK

OUR WORLD IS IN A STATE OF SUFFERING. CHRISTIANS WOULD AGREE that Jesus is the answer. However, could it be possible that the church, as a whole, is limiting the activity of God within our lives and communities? Could we be hindering God's work by our own willful disobedience?

Allow me to paint a sad picture:

Mr. and Mrs. Christian (a fictitious couple) are both very sick with heart disease, hypertension, and type 2 diabetes. They spend a good amount of money each month on medications and doctors' visits. Routinely they visit the prayer line at church to have a minister lay hands upon and pray over them. They are so out of energy and have gained so much weight that both their community engagement and physical mobility have suffered. They truly want to serve the Lord but are routinely hindered by their physical maladies.

What is the real issue with Mr. and Mrs. Christian? Is it the wrong medications? Bad doctors? Not enough faith? Unanswered prayers?

I must tell you that the answer is none of the above. Their choices, and snowballing effects, are the primary cause, along with the standard American lifestyle and western diet. Do we judge Mr. and Mrs. Christian? Certainly not. Society, and even prevailing church culture, fosters ignorance.

We need a change and healing of the heart. This will lead to healing of the body. Two scriptures are worth noting:

2 Chronicles 7:14: "If My people who are called by My name will humble themselves, and pray and seek My face, and turn from their wicked ways, then I will hear from heaven, and will forgive their sin and heal their land."

(Note: I believe the word "land" in the verse above applies to our bodies.)

Matthew 21:12-14: "Then Jesus went into the temple of God and drove out all those who bought and sold in the temple and overturned the tables of the money changers and the seats of those who sold doves. And He said to them, 'It is written, 'My house shall be called a house of prayer,' but you have made it a den of thieves.' Then the blind and the lame came to Him in the temple, and He healed them."

(Note: After Jesus drove out the money changers *from* the temple, the blind and the lame were healed *in* the temple. Could this be symbolic of our body?)

My friend, I'm encouraging repentance, a change to the right direction, for *your* well-being. We cannot continue ignoring (rebelling against) the obvious. Too many people have failed to care for their temples, allowed the worldly culture to shape us, and asked God to fix our mistakes without repenting. This is a false use of grace that leads to disappointment and confusion.

If this applies to you, make a simple turn in the right direction today. Allow God to display his healing power in our lives as a testimony the world cannot deny.

85
The Best Time

DR. MICHELE

My grandfather told us kids, who had a tendency to sleep too long in the morning, that "The morning is the best time of the day!"

Being a farmer, milking cows and doing other chores before breakfast forced his early wake-up time. Think about it, he learned the worth of the morning by engaging inactivities which made it so worthwhile. The Psalmist, evidently, experienced a similar discovery in Psalm 5:3,

> "Give ear to my words, O Lord; give heed to my sighing! Listen to the sound of my cry, my King and my God; for to You, I pray. O Lord, in the morning You hear my voice. In the morning, I plead my case to You, and watch."

We often hear someone suggest a product with the encouragement of, "Just try it and see." Grandpa "tried it" as did the Psalmist and discovered the worth of doing special things in the morning, so as to enjoy "the best part of the day."

The day seems to go better when we start off with some exercise, a run, and coffee. Why not make sure that morning time with the Lord is a part of that program? Time with Him, our Creator and Savior, assure us that no matter what happens, the day will be the best that it can be.

There are so many ways we can invest time with God: pondering His Word, singing our praise and worship to Him, praying, and asking how we can be a blessing to others today.

Like Grandpa and the Psalmist, "we watch" and discover that it works! What a difference the Lord makes in every day! All - courtesy of Jesus. He makes the connections!

86
God's Presence In This Moment

DR. MICHELE

TODAY, RIGHT NOW, LET'S TAKE A FEW MINUTES AND REMIND OURSELVES of the realties of God's healing power within our spirit.

Your spirit is united with Jesus, no ifs, ands or buts. (1 Corinthians 6:17) Whoever is united with the Lord is one with him in spirit, and everything that flows in Him right now is flowing in your spirit right now. Yes, right now.

Get quieter.

He never leaves us or forsakes us. Never.

This ever present healing power is palpable, always! This means we need to be present, ever more present, with His Spirit.

Within you is a medicine. Mark 5:30 says, "And Jesus, immediately knowing in Himself that power had gone out of Him, turned around in the crowd and said, 'Who touched My clothes?'" That medicine is God's power and love.

When people receive a prescription for medication, they usually take it daily. But do we "take" in all God offers on a daily basis? Let us never forget where the healing source comes from!

Gods word tells us that the same power that raised up Jesus from the dead is alive and working in our mortal bodies. Call upon him, pray, and cooperate with the right actions.

> "But if the Spirit of Him who raised Jesus from the dead dwells in you, He who raised Christ from the dead will also give life to your mortal bodies through His Spirit who dwells in you." (ROMANS 8:11)

We hope you will spend time with God right now, and and know His healing power and love.

87
Dangers of the Comfort Zone

DR. MARK

It's easy to become addicted to comfort, ease, and pleasure in the modern world. But according to a recent article in a psychology magazine, there are significant dangers to staying in the comfort zone too long.

Bottom line: "if you can't step out of your comfort zone you may experience difficulty making change or transitioning, growing, and ultimately, transforming; in other words, all those things that define who you are and give your life meaning."

This principle is critical to our spiritual growth and maturity. Moreover, if we do not grow spiritually mature, we will repeat childish behaviors that get us into hot water. Allow me to explain with scripture.

Exodus 16:2-4: "In the desert the whole community grumbled against Moses and Aaron. The Israelites said to them, 'If only we had died by the Lord's hand in Egypt! There we sat around pots of meat and ate all the food we wanted, but you have brought us out into this desert to starve this entire assembly to death.' Then the Lord said to Moses, 'I will rain down bread from heaven for you. The people are to go out each day and gather enough for that day. In this way I will test them and see whether they will follow my instructions."

Allow me to paraphrase this sentiment from the Israelites: "We were content in Egypt. Why did you drag us out here? Dying there would have been fine. Even though we had no freedom, we ate all we wanted and had steady work. That was way better than chasing this 'promised land' thing."

The Israelites were stuck. They had lost their ability to transition, grow, and transform. They were more comfortable with the past than pressing into a brighter future.

Today, we as the body of Christ are cautioned to inventory where we are and what we are doing.

Are things staying the same and are we growing?

Are we making positive changes spiritually, emotionally, and physically?

Are we making childish mistakes that continue to cost us.

The comfort zone is nice, but it can become *too* comfortable. Let's allow the Israelites' actions and attitudes serve as a reminder that it is easy to get stuck in captivity, and enjoy it. The truth is, the narrow road is ultimately the best and most enjoyable.

88
The True Treasure

DR. MICHELE

Today's thoughts came when reading this scripture from 2 Timothy 1:14.

> *"Guard the good treasure entrusted to you with the help of the Holy Spirit living in us."*

Sounds like we have received a treasure that must be guarded, but we have a "guard helper" in the Holy Spirit. What does the treasure consist of? Another Scripture brings light, from 2 Corinthians 9:8,14.

> *"God is able to provide you with every blessing in abundance...*
> *the surpassing grace of God that He has given you."*

And thus from 2 Corinthians 12:9:

> *"My grace is sufficient for you."*

Grace. What a priceless treasure! As Ephesians 2:8 informs us:

> *"By grace you have been saved through faith, and this is not your own doing. It is the gift of God."*

So then, God has deposited sufficient good treasure in our account in His "Grace Bank." By the way, that happened by what Jesus made available through His redeeming love in action. He purchased our "treasure" when dying in our behalf. Such treasure is secure in His "bank." It will never go broke, even though we hear of neighborhood banks and other financial institutions going belly up. His bank always stays open, and we can make withdrawals 24/7!

That said, we still can misuse those grace treasures with foolish living, or fail to "draw" on our account by ignoring time with God.

Today, let us guard our accounts by enlightening our minds and empowering our wills to live smart in a stupid world!

89
Our Good Shepherd

DR. MICHELE

STARTING AT BIRTH, WE HUMANS NEED CARE, SOMEONE TO MEET OUR daily needs. The analogy of shepherd and sheep comes to mind. Let's reflect on these Scriptures:

> "Then Micaiah the prophet answered: 'I saw all Israel scattered on the hills like sheep without a shepherd.'" (2 CHRONICLES 18:16)

> "We all like sheep have gone astray. Each of us has turned to His own way, and the Lord has laid on Him the iniquity of us all." (Isaiah 53:6)

> "I am the good Shepherd. I know My sheep and they know Me... I lay down My life for the sheep... My sheep listen to My voice. I know them and they follow Me. I give them eternal life... No one can snatch them out of My hand. (JOHN 10:14-15, 27-28)

Many have characterized sheep as not the brightest of creatures, drawing a parallel between sheep and people. Well, look how easily we can be lead astray into the wrong ways of thinking, believing, and living. How often do we wander in the wrong direction or follow the wrong crowd. We're very familiar with our conscience troubling us, right?

That's where Jesus comes in! If He becomes our Shepherd, He alone knows the right way to the good pasture. As we follow His leading, we learn to recognize His voice and to truly appreciate His way of caring for us, and for all of His flock.

He proved His care for you and me by laying down His life to provide it!

Being one of His sheep, we can feel "safe and secure from all alarm" as one Gospel hymn states. Yes, real security, even with our tendency to go astray.

But, how do we hear His voice? He speaks through His Holy Word, which we know as the Bible. By His teaching Spirit, we "hear" His voice, and take to heart

His message.

Let Jesus be our "Shepherd," stay in His "pasture" with His "flock," where we can be secure, hear His voice, and then following where His voice guides!

That's what Mark Sherwood and I plan and pray to continue doing, and we trust that's your plan and prayer, also.

Live the "Wellness" life with us! We believe in you!

90
What do Health and Pastors have in Common?

DR. MARK

I know, the title of this reading might seem strange. But let's start by first defining "pastor" with Biblical context.

A pastor is a faithful steward. (Titus 1:7) The term used is overseer (the Greek word: episkopos). It's a functional title of the elder. He is a steward, a manager of God's resources and of Jesus' flock.

The word "pastor" actually came from the word found in Latin that means "shepherd" which, in turn, originated from the verb "pascere" which means "to set to grazing, lead to pasture, cause to eat." (Most of the time this imagery is used as a metaphor, but you might still encounter churches where a lot of "grazing" is encouraged.)

According to 1 Timothy 3:2, an overseer has to be temperate, respectable, above reproach, self-controlled, able to teach and, most importantly, faithful to his wife.

> Let's focus on the shepherd and pasture. Psalm 23 comes to mind:
> "The Lord is my shepherd; I shall not want.
> He makes me to lie down in green pastures;
> He leads me beside the still waters.
> He restores my soul;
> He leads me in the paths of righteousness for His name's sake.
> Yea, though I walk through the valley of the shadow of death, I will fear no evil; For You are with me; Your rod and Your staff, they comfort me.
> You prepare a table before me in the presence of my enemies; You anoint my head with oil; My cup runs over.

Surely goodness and mercy shall follow me all the days of my life; And I will dwell in the house of the Lord forever."

Now let's examine "green pastures" and "still waters." This means the pastor/shepherd leads people towards health (green pastures and still waters are God's provision). The pastor is equipped to lead people to God's supply. Contrast that to the world's supply of poor food and drink that leads to disease processes.

So here are some hard but appropriate questions:

Should a pastor speak to his flock about physical health? Should a pastor lead by example in health? Should a pastor protect the flock, when able, from poor food and lifestyle choices?

The answer, my dear friend is *yes*.

Consider these two truths:

1. The flock will only go in the right direction as far as the shepherd leads
2. The bar will only be set as high as the leader is willing to set it.

91
No Lack of Blessings

DR. MICHELE

There are many times when it seems like there's something lacking: time, energy, money, wisdom, and the list goes on. We can get tied up in lack! Our seeming lack can drop us into a state of despair.

James 1:2 speaks to this:

> "Consider it pure joy, my brothers, whenever you face trials of many kinds."

Finding joy in trials and tribulations isn't always easy but it allows us to count our blessings. We can see how rich we truly are. Acknowledge the "simple" things, like food, shelter, and clothing. We often forget these blessings, and especially the biggest blessing: Being a child of the King.

In all things we are to latch onto the opportunity to depend upon God. The truth is that self-sufficiency is a myth perpetuated by pride and temporary success. Health and wealth can disappear instantly, as can life itself. In fact, life itself is one grand gift.

Begin today concentrating your efforts on God and staying present in the moment, grateful for what you *do* have. Being overly focused on lack robs the sensations of what is true in the moment.

2 Corinthians 12:9 reminds us, "And he said to me, 'My grace is sufficient for you, for power is perfected in weakness.' Most gladly, therefore, I will rather boast about my weaknesses, so that the power of Christ may dwell in me."

Counting our blessings every day will overcome the spirit of lack! Invest some time remembering how blessed you are today.

92

Spiritual Supplements

DR. MICHELE

Here's a thought about receiving communion. Mark and I take a few vitamin supplements. And some of my patients need medication for certain conditions. Some medications address more critical issues than others. All are important for what they do, and we believe they deposit their health benefit to us.

Amazing, indeed, that they go where they need to go, and do what they're prescribed to do. Supplements, when used correctly, allow our metabolic engines to run a little faster, and cleaner.

Jesus instituted what we call The Lord's Supper on the occasion of the Jewish Passover celebration. He told them:

> "'I have eagerly desired to eat this Passover with you before I suffer.' And, then followed: 'This is My body which is given for you. Do this in remembrance of Me… This cup is the new covenant in My Blood. Do this as often as you drink it in remembrance of Me.'" (I Corinthians 11:24-25)

The Passover event for the Jew recalled the blessings every Jewish household received when the angel of death "passed over" their homes upon seeing the blood of a spotless
lamb applied to their doorposts. In communion, we receive a healthy dose of spiritual "medication" for the soul to keep us spiritually healthy. We believe and receive, with bread and wine, the benefits promised and freely given to us through the Blood of Jesus, the spotless Lamb of God. Receiving such, we maintain a healthy spiritual and mental condition.

I can't explain how this happens, but Jesus promises that it truly does. So, as Mark and I share in communion, we know that we receive a "health benefit" similar to that as when we take our supplements.

We both pray and trust that you will also believe in what Jesus gives you in communion: assurance of forgiveness, daily grace, a living hope of eternal life, and more.

Just as you do with what a doctor prescribes, both "supplements" require faith.

Additionally, every time we intently read the Bible, and mix the Word with faith, the benefits of heaven improve our mental and spiritual health as well. Truly, our Great Physician knows how to provide for us, His patients!

93
Moses Today

DR. MARK

As I was pondering on Moses' incredible life, I was struck by several aspects:
1. He felt often ill-equipped.
2. He continued to press forward through discouragement.
3. He had an unwavering love for his people.
4. His love for and obedience to God was uncompromising.

I bet he felt frustrated regarding the situation described in Exodus 16:2-3.

> *"Then the whole congregation of the children of Israel complained against Moses and Aaron in the wilderness. And the children of Israel said to them, 'Oh, that we had died by the hand of the Lord in the land of Egypt, when we sat by the pots of meat and when we ate bread to the full! For you have brought us out into this wilderness to kill this whole assembly with hunger.'"*

Here we see clearly that even though Israel was out of bondage, they inwardly wanted to return to enslavement. What a crazy dilemma! But is this an unusual scenario? Let's apply this reasoning to a real world situation.

Today's public health is at an all-time low. And sadly, this does include the church. The vast majority of the diseases that plague us now are literally self-created we willingly participate in the standard American diet, lifestyle, and culture. I call this SAD (standard American diet). We all know we need to eat better, exercise more, stress less, and sleep more. But so many of us don't. Why?

As in Moses' day, the masses seem to prefer bondage to freedom. Every day, Dr. Michele and I stand on various "platforms" and preach, "Get out of captivity now. This lifestyle is killing you. Come with us, and we will show you the way to freedom!"

Some allow us to lead them out to the "promised land" where there is freedom from many drugs, obesity, bad habits, and disease processes. But sadly, many don't. This brings us to tears, literally, on many occasions as we grieve for people.

So, because of our care for you, we ask these questions boldly:

Are you in bondage to the SAD now?

If so, do you really want to be free?

If the answer is yes, it's time to venture to the land of freedom. This journey will not be easy, so keep your eye on the reward and blessing!

94

Running the Race

DR. MICHELE

EVERY RACE NEEDS A TRACK TO RUN ON, WHETHER IT'S A TRACK EVENT, the Kentucky Derby, or the Indy 500. And most race facilities have room for an audience. Consider this scripture:

> *"Since we are surrounded by so great a cloud of witnesses, let us lay aside every weight and the sin that clings so closely and let us run with perseverance the race that is set before us, looking to Jesus the pioneer and perfecter of our faith, who for the sake of the joy set before Him, endured the cross, disregarding its shame, and has taken His seat at the right hand of the throne of God."* (HEBREWS 12:1-2)

We admit that we're people "on the go." Going and doing as soon as our feet hit the floor in the morning. But where are we going, and what are we doing? The above passage reveals also that our going and doing can be likened to our being on a track and in a race.

Days and years make up the track, and our life is in the race. Like any runner, we "dress" for this kind of race. Whatever may hamper doing our best needs to be removed. (Sin is heavy and makes for losers.)

We humans seem to be created with a craving to win and be successful. Winning demands much discipline and sweat, total commitment.

The above Scripture offers quite a lesson for us Christians. "Lay aside every weight of sin… run with perseverance… looking to Jesus" our super coach. We run with the stadium filled with the family of God, cheering us to victory.

And what "prize" can be expected? Along with being "seated" with Jesus, by His Grace, we can hear a "well done" from our Father in Heaven. Wow.

Pause and consider that for a moment.

The more we consider the eternal outcome of our race, the more motivated we will be to lay aside every weight and hinderance.

95
Abuse of God's Grace

DR. MARK

Did you know that grace that can be properly used, or negatively abused?

First, let's truly define grace. Grace is the free, undeserved, and unlimited gift of forgiveness and even benevolence. Grace does not expect anything in return. It is given without strings, from a place of love.

How can we abuse grace? Does that even seem possible? Let's first begin by analyzing a very well-known scripture:

> *"For by grace you have been saved through faith, and that not of yourselves; it is the gift of God, not of works, lest anyone should boast."* (Ephesians 2:8-9 NKJV)

Here we see grace, in its proper context, clearly defined. This grace is given freely by God, to his people, as a result of faith. We should point out that both are given without any framework as to our behavior or works. In other words, our works have nothing to do with the gifts of grace and faith.

This brings us to the improper application of grace. Abused grace is much like a license to commit a crime without concern of consequence.

Clearly, we saw what to do in the life of Jesus. After being tempted for forty days in the desert, Jesus was tested with the opportunity to jump off the temple. He was told by the devil that angels would catch Him and prevent harm. We know, that if Jesus wanted, He could've jumped, and indeed, the angels would have caught him. However, why jump? That would have been putting God in an odd position, that being a God Who saves us in moments of intentional foolishness.

Sure, we will make goofy decisions from time to time, but isn't this much like purposefully walking in front of a bus, expecting the bus not to hit you, expecting God to restore and heal us? Isn't that the way we think sometimes? *We can do want we want, regardless of the circumstances, and expect God to fix it.* This, my friends, is a misapplication, misuse, and even abuse of grace.

Let's apply this to our physical health. We continue to consume various substances we know are extremely harmful and have nothing but negative consequences for our body. These things could be categorized as the following: sodas, fried foods, sugars, and processed foods.

We all know these will hurt us, right? We are not so foolish to believe these are healthy, are we? Then why, oh why, would we put them in our bodies knowing fully they contribute heavily to disease processes that may shorten our lifespan. Are we expecting God to heal our bodies, when we actually contributed to the illness?

As one can clearly see, we all have opportunities to make choices throughout life. Generally speaking, if we listen to the Holy Spirit, we will know what choices to make. However, we would be remiss if we did not mention the possibility that we will likely sin, by driving through red lights.

This is the battle we face daily. It is the battle between the spirit and the flesh. Friend, we should not yield to the flesh on a routine basis in a willful manner. This will only yield consequences that affect every area of our life, including our physical health. By expecting God to continue to correct consequences brought about by our own repetitive choices, which we know are clearly in error, we are absolutely putting ourselves in a position of abuse of grace.

Though this is a hard subject matter, it is one in that warrants serious thought. Let's all reflect on the question, *Am I repetitively abusing God's grace?*

96
True Colors

DR. MICHELE

I LOVE PRACTICING MEDICINE, YET SOMETIMES IT CAN BE CHALLENGING. No matter what profession you are in, or who you are, we have days that press us, right?

And those days are when we get to "see our true colors" as they say.

When the days seem long and hard, and disappointment rings your bell, a few scriptures come to mind:

"Put on God's whole armor [the armor of a heavy-armed soldier which God supplies], that you may be able successfully to stand up against [all] the strategies and the deceits of the devil." (Ephesians 6:11 AMP)

We are only here for such a short time and somehow we continually put our faith in the wrong things. When things don't work out, we have to stop and reevaluate.

What?! You mean what I had planned was not God's plan?

Nope, it was my plan! I somehow got distracted from His plan. Do we enjoy the disappointment? Do we enjoy the redirection? Of course not, but if we listen and follow in those situations, transformation takes place!

Another scripture resonates.

> *"Be still, and know (recognize and understand) that I am God. I will be exalted among the nations! I will be exalted in the earth!"* (PSALM 46:10 AMP)

Silence (being still before God) can be hard when we want answers, when we're disappointed, or when our mind wants to run a million miles an hour! Perhaps our almighty Father knows we need a much needed break!

Silence can be deafening or edifying. Sometimes the silence can be quiet enough to hear a pin drop. If His voice is softer than that, we have to come to the point of complete stillness to hear.

Let's learn to be quiet. The voice of God is always there.

97
What is our Purpose?

DR. MARK

I am sure we've all asked ourselves, "Why am I here?" or "What is my purpose?"

Do not feel bad about asking. These questions can promote introspection and beneficial recalibration of direction in life.

When I think of purpose, I am led directly to the great commission (a word directly from Jesus to his disciples).

> "Then the eleven disciples went to Galilee, to the mountain where Jesus had told them to go. When they saw him, they worshiped him; but some doubted. Then Jesus came to them and said, "All authority in heaven and on earth has been given to me. Therefore, go and make disciples of all nations, baptizing them in the name of the Father and of the Son and of the Holy Spirit, and teaching them to obey everything I have commanded you. And surely, I am with you always, to the very end of the age."
> (Matthew 28:16-20)

"Commission" has the idea of a board or committee. Therefore, the committee or group includes anyone who is a true follower of Jesus. The disciple then will apply what he has learned and teach others. And so, we conclude, the disciples were given the "committee" assignment to go, make disciples, teach, and baptize.

As I ponder this directive, I am reinvigorated with the clear concept of purpose. If we claim to be disciples, we should exhibit the disciplines of our teacher and then demonstrate those disciplines and the fruits therein to the world, all to God's glory.

So, I ask, are we "going"? Are we "making disciples"? Are we "teaching"? Are we "baptizing"? (And as someone who speaks about physical health, we must remember that no one can do any of these things if one is dead. Let's honor the temple (our body) and treat it with care as God's precious creation.)

Our purpose is tied to what Jesus "did" for us, and what we "do" with his grace and provision. If we truly embrace the purpose, we must also embrace the process and not destroy our lives, one neglectful bite or decision at a time.

What we eat, do, say, and think impact our effectiveness in fulfilling God's purpose in our lives. He gives us discipline and authority from His throne to reside in our heart so that we, as his disciples, can "go, make, teach, and baptize."

98
Faithfulness

DR. MICHELE

Life can seem really sporadic.

In spite of this observation, I strive to be more faithful. But as I do, my thoughts can become sporadic and my train of thought goes off the rails. How about you?

I believe faithfulness deserves some quality time to ponder as an important characteristic in our lives. Everyday, whether we are a parent, child, student, employee, business owner, CEO, political leader, craftsman, teacher, or doctor, faithfulness ought to be a key factor in who we are and what we do.

How dependable, faithful, and trustworthy am I? Scriptures come to mind.

"Forever, O Lord, Your Word is settled in heaven. Your faithfulness endures to all generations!" (Psalm 119:90)

As His children, God's faithfulness should inspire us to be like Him in every way possible. Scripture also informs us of the faithfulness of Jesus:

"Consider the Apostle and High Priest of our confession, Christ Jesus, who was faithful to Him who appointed Him..." (Hebrews 3:1-2)

Shouldn't we who have been forgiven, born again, and saved by grace thank Jesus for His faithfulness "even unto death" for our sakes? Shouldn't we be like Him in faithfulness in all areas of our lives as He was, "even unto death"? To the Church at Smyrna, Jesus made a promise:

"Be faithful unto death and I will give you the crown of life." (Revelation 2:10)

Let's aim for life-long faithfulness, and look for opportunities to be faithful today.

99
I Wander and Wonder

DR. MICHELE

Have you ever wondered why the mind wanders? It is like a gerbil on a wheel, often taking us nowhere, or to places we do not want to go.

"Be careful how you think; your life is shaped by your thoughts."
(Proverbs 4:23)

If we are not careful, items that hold no weight will get in our minds and take up space. When the hard drive is full of negatives, there is no room to experience the joy of the moment. We can become deaf to Gods plan for us, and miss out on blessing.

Think the same way Jesus thought, Philippians 2:5 encourages us.

Jesus knew the world was misguided, and He loved anyway. He was constantly providing a way for people to transform their focus. We must continue to be on guard against the ways of the world and the negativity that bombards our minds.

"There must be spiritual renewal of your thoughts and attitudes"
(Ephesians 4:23)

Step off the gerbil wheel. Enjoy the day. Be love, and love always.

100
Where Oh Where is the Healing?

DR. MARK

As we see disease trends growing throughout the world, I am even more saddened by the same trends being very visible in the church. The worst part of this trend is that the majority of these diseases are self-imposed and choice-driven.

Wait a minute Mark, you cannot be serious. We love God and live for Him, we are not really choosing to be sick, are we?

Certainly, not all sickness and disease occurs because of one's choice. Let's be clear about this, and our commitment to bring compassion to everyone facing health challenges.

With many people we encounter, it grieves me to say that indeed, our choices are shortening our lives (and effectiveness) on earth. Remember, Jesus healed people. We should too. And we as people should walk healed as well.

But what is stopping us? Could it be our lack of faith? As we read in Mark 6:1-6:

"Jesus left there and went to his hometown, accompanied by his disciples. When the Sabbath came, he began to teach in the synagogue, and many who heard him were amazed. 'Where did this man get these things?' they asked. 'What's this wisdom that has been given him? What are these remarkable miracles he is performing? Isn't this the carpenter? Isn't this Mary's son and the brother of James, Joseph, Judas and Simon? Aren't his sisters here with us?' And they took offense at him. Jesus said to them, 'A prophet is not without honor except in his own town, among his relatives and in his own home.' He could not do any miracles there, except lay his hands on a few sick people and heal them. He was amazed at their lack of faith."

It is astonishing that even Jesus' desire to heal was thwarted by individual's unbelief and lack of faith.

My wife and I have definitely felt the grief of seeing people not get well because they simply refused to believe. But I'm glad to report that we see healing routinely occur in people across the globe. I know God heals.

I am boldly calling on the church to rethink healing, faith, and personal responsibility. We have a part to play. Faith is an action that requires us to do the right things, eat the way God intended, move physically, and understand that we as people have a part to play in healing.

Jesus is not a genie in a bottle who grants our wishes. He is the Lord who chooses to make His home in each of us. Yes, we need healing physically, but folks, we need healing emotionally and spiritually too from deceptive teachings and incomplete doctrine.

Build your belief on His Word, today!

101
Hearing and Listening

DR. MICHELE

Thank God for the ability to hear! However, how we process what we hear depends upon what information we have stored in our "computer minds." True hearing consists of more than sound bites.

Let's "listen" to this Scripture:

"Be doers of the word and not merely hearers, who deceive themselves." (James 1:22)

Words shape thoughts, and thoughts process what's heard, hopefully discerning and understanding the true meaning of those words. If not, we can miss the blessings those words intended to convey.

Once we accept the words and process them properly, the meanings come through and we act on them. How many times have we shut out the words we hear? As children, we can shut out the words of parents, teachers, and others in authority? Adults are no better when what we hear doesn't please our minds and emotions.

It's also true that some statements heard don't deserve our time, or may be harmful if really taken to heart. However, when our loving heavenly Father wants a word with us, we should by all means hear and apply it. He only wants good for us.

"Let anyone who hears, listen." (Matt. 11:15)

No one has more important words to share with us than He who died for us and pleads with us! We should tune out what isn't worth our time, and makes sure to listen to the truth Jesus wants us to hear and live by.

I pray that we will always have open ears to hear what Jesus is saying. His words bring life at its best!

102

Conforming to His Way

DR. MICHELE

Today the word "conform" comes to mind. This word has a variety of similar meanings, and a scripture passage brought it to my mind:

> "Be not conformed to this world, but be transformed by the renewing of your minds; so that you may discern what is of God - what is good and acceptable and perfect." (ROMANS 12:2)

In every period of time, including the present, we humans realize that the good and the bad coexist on earth. Which of these shape our lives depends on which we conform to.

What we go along with, agree to, or subscribe to shapes us. This verse makes a strong appeal: "Be not conformed to this world, but be transformed"!

Thus, we have a choice: conform to this world, or conform to the will and Word of God.

> "Do not love the world or the things in the world. The love of the Father is not in those who love the world; for all that is in the world—the desire of the flesh, the desire of the eyes, the pride in riches—comes not from the Father but from the world. And the world and its desire are passing away, but those who do the will of God live forever." (I JOHN 2:15-17)

I get it! What the world offers with its enticing appeals won't benefit, especially in the long run. But what our loving God offers blesses life in the moment and eternally.

Good reason then to go God's way as provided for us by all that Jesus did in our behalf.

Remember, Jesus said: "I am the way the truth and the life, no one comes to the Father except by Me." We can't go wrong going His way!

103
Is Change a Challenge?

DR. MARK

Bringing change is not that difficult.

In all of our travel, in our clinic, and at speaking engagements we hear a repeated theme. "I know I should not do this." "I need to do better." "I know this is bad for me."

These statements are related to our poor lifestyle choices, consuming foods that are not food, but in fact very deadly, as well as drinking sugary, disease-causing beverages.

Actually, change is not that hard. Let me explain.

"But the fruit of the Spirit is love, joy, peace, patience, kindness, goodness, faithfulness, gentleness, self-control; against such things there is no law." (Galatians 5:22-23)

I am sure you realize these are the fruits (outcomes, characteristics) of the presence of the Spirit (The Holy Spirit, the person and presence of God) living in you. If you really believe this, it simply means that in you, you have all the characteristics of God, which can be manifest in and through you simply by acknowledging his presence.

That's right, we do not have to ask for the things we already have. You can choose rightly, conquer temptation, and be a blessed steward of your temple!

With that established, making changes is as simple as 1, 2, 3.

1. Consume foods that are anti-inflammatory and non-disease causing/contributing. Here is a list:
    a. Quality proteins: organic, grass fed and finished, free range, wild caught.

    b. Healthy oils and fats: olive oil, coconut oil, avocado, nuts, seeds
    c. Low glycemic fruits: berries, oranges, apples
    d. Low glycemic non-root, non-starchy vegetables

2. Avoid foods that are inflammatory and disease causing/contributing. Here is a list:
    a. Sugars/artificial sweeteners
    b. Fried foods
    c. Processed foods
    d. Sodas
    e. Excess caffeine and alcohol
    f. Refined breads and grains
    g. Soy
    h. Corn

3. Trust God to supply all your needs (food, shelter, clothing) and embrace the "fruits" of God within you (especially self-control).

That's it. Simple as 1, 2, 3.

Remember the majority of prayer lines in America are filled with folks who have chosen to follow the standard American lifestyle. It is not because of bad genes. It is because of bad choices.

Let's choose God today and trust His power in us to make positive changes that become permanent.

104

Who Will Rescue?

DR. MICHELE

SOME THINGS WE WISH WEREN'T REALITIES. ONE MAJOR REALITY stems from a serious condition of our flesh that causes us to do stuff that we shouldn't. This includes the struggles we have within our thoughts and various temptations.

Temptations stimulate such battles and our conscience raises a red flag. However, we often yield. Why is it so easy to get off track even when we know our actions will cause harm?

Such inner battles the Apostle Paul wrote about in Romans 7:19-25.

"I do not do the good I want, but the evil I do not want is what I do… Who will rescue me?"

To which he answers, "Thanks be to God through Jesus Christ our Lord!"

We expect rescue in the face of wrong action. How is that logical? How's this possible? Only by the love of our Savior.

We all face the same inner struggles and must constantly maintain our obedience. Yes, obedience is a tough word. If we look at the state of our world today, the problems stem from the lack of obedience to God in the face of the inner struggles of the heart.

Let's get real. When we get ourselves in line, peace ensues! Why do we refuse to manage our own behavior?

Recently, something from the old comic strip, "Peanuts" came to my attention. It seems that Lucy, the older sister of Linus, drew him a picture of the human heart. Her depiction was half white and half black. When showing him what she drew, she got theological and told him that a battle goes on in our hearts. Linus replied that he felt the battle. We may smile about his reply, but we also know its reality. *Been there and done that!*

However, we have hope and we have help. Jesus' life, death, and resurrection gives cause for rejoicing. "Thanks be to God through Jesus Christ our Lord." He rescues! He heals the sin-sick heart! He delivers from what tempts us!

We can count on Him, and come to Him, and that's an expression of faith. And He does expect us to correct our wrong action. Correct the problem and experience the miracle!

Today, ask to be set free from our fleshly, sinful ways and the temptations that bug us. We know we can't do it alone and are thankful to be connected to the power that can!

105
Wounds from a Friend

DR. MARK

FRIEND, DO WE WANT TO SEE AND ENJOY A MINISTRY OF HEALING OR business as usual?

In over three decades of involvement in ministry and health, I have observed many trends and changes in society, some of which are very concerning.

1. Obesity is the fasting-growing, non-communicable disease worldwide.
2. The subject of health (especially, lifestyle choices) is mostly ignored in the church.
3. We continue to routinely use "non-foods" to draw people to church gatherings.
4. Diseases in the US are growing at a faster rate than the growth of the population as a whole.

While these trends are probably not shocking, let me make a point very clear. I am pleading with you right now to hear God's perspective to each of the above four.

1. The disease of obesity is the result of gluttony, food worship, addiction, and mostly willful destruction of God's best creation (the body = the temple)
2. To fail to address health is equivalent to denying Christ's commands to honor the temple and heal the sick.
3. To use non-foods (processed grains and sugars, GMO, and basically anything not created in the form by God) is to allow the great imitator and copycat (Satan) to control your choices and

wreak havoc on your health, by refusing to allow God to supply what your body needs to flourish.
4. If diseases are growing so fast, why is sickness in the church mirroring the trend? Doesn't God want us to be the healthiest people on planet earth, to be different and peculiar as a way to bring glory to Himself?

These points may be somewhat challenging to accept or even discuss. However, Jesus did not veer from difficult subjects for fear of political correctness or loss of followers. It is the truth that sets one free. Lies (overt, covert, or omission) keep people in bondage.

God's call is clear: "Free my people. Free them from bondage. It is courage I give you to lead their escape. Be free to truly experience me."

Proverbs 27:6 (NLT) says, "Wounds from a sincere friend are better than many kisses from an enemy."

106
A Stronghold of True Blessings

DR. MICHELE

I was sitting down in the quiet last evening, spending time in the Word, following a *long* week. Whenever I do this, I am always reminded of my many blessings!

This time I realized how blessed I am to be married to a man who continually speaks life into my life. We all know it is not good to focus on our heartaches, tragedies, and pain, but sometimes fear, resentment, anger, unforgiveness, and disappointment take over, no matter how well balanced we believe ourselves to be. My sweet husband always knows what to say and how to stand by my side to keep the Word of God alive in me, and my faith refreshed.

No matter who we are, the trials and tribulations of our previous experiences resonate in our nervous system, embedded in the barracks of our minds just waiting for a moment to show themselves. When life gets a little stressful, we become fatigued and pressured, and that negativity tries to run our lives.

If we are not careful the spirit of fear (False Evidence Appearing Real) will entrench in our minds and hearts. I was reminded by the comforting words of my sweetheart just moments ago and I wish to remind you!

"The Lord did not give us a spirit of fear, but of love, power and a sound mind." (2 Timothy 1:7) The fact that there is a comma and a "but" in that verse tells us that the second half trumps the first! Let's evaluate more deeply.

The Lord did not give us a spirit of fear. The comma cancels that spirit of fear! The second statement about power, love, and a strong mind is the truth. If we are truly living from that standpoint, fear has no foothold in our lives. But when we get entangled with humanly thinking, being, and doing, before we know it we are overloaded with the negative thoughts and emotions. This negativity comes from allowing the father of lies (Satan) to take a foothold in our thinking.

Sometimes the pressures of life get to me! My sweet husband not only can see it on my face, but feel it in my being when that spirit of fear tries to mess with me. Thankfully, the man stands by my side and brings me back to the centerline quicker than one can blink an eye. He is quick to guide me back to Scripture.

How could I ever forget Psalm 23?

"The Lord is my Shepherd, I shall not want." (I lack nothing.)

Living in the spirit of fear contradicts this passage. I now carry this scripture on a piece of paper and pull it out of my pocket many times a day. I find myself reading it not only to myself, but to my patients and others in need.

I am blessed by the hand of the man, and the heart of the man, I hold! I am even more blessed by his strong hold to our Father in heaven!

Live the wellness life today. A life of power, love, and a sound mind!

107
Nutritional guidelines for healing

DR. MARK

"Don't you know that you yourselves are God's temple and that God's Spirit dwells in your midst?" (1 Corinthians 3:16)

Friend, your body is God's temple. Pause and consider this truth for a moment.

Later in his letter to the Corinthians, Paul goes on to say,

> "'I have the right to do anything,' you say—but not everything is beneficial. 'I have the right to do anything'—but I will not be mastered by anything. ... Do you not know that your bodies are temples of the Holy Spirit, who is in you, whom you have received from God? You are not your own; you were bought at a price. Therefore honor God with your bodies." (1 Corinthians 6:12, 19-20)

How do we honor God with our bodies?

We are often asked to provide dietary guidelines and protocols to our community. We get asked questions such as,

"Which diet is best? Should I eat for my blood type? How many carbohydrates, proteins, and fat should I consume? How many calories should I eat?"

With that as our backdrop, allow me to address these head on.

First, diets *do not* work. Dieting is a bad idea. Never go on a diet.

Second, counting calories for dietary guidance is faulty as this science has been disproven. A calorie is not a calorie equally to each person.

Third, counting calories, and consequently lowering caloric intake on the belief that that will cause weight loss, will lower your metabolic rate and produce less energy, which is counterproductive to our purpose.

And fourth, *never* use weight loss as a target to health. Scale weight tells you nothing. It is body composition that tells you everything.

For those wanting 100% success with nutrition, and consequently, a better bodily healing process, here are some sure-fire guidelines that will work for you:

1. Eliminate all breads, sugars, rice, processed foods, fried foods, sodas, soy, and corn.
2. Consume unlimited amounts of above-ground vegetables including spinach, kale, cauliflower, broccoli, field greens, collard greens, and the like. This would also include anything that basically grows above the ground as a vegetable.
3. Limit fruit to two half-cup servings per day.
4. Use the following guidelines when selecting protein: grass fed and grass finished, hormone and antibiotic free, wild caught, free range, and organic.
5. Consume generous amounts of healthy fats including: olive oil, avocado, macadamia, and coconut oil.

These guideline will produce positive results. Don't believe it? Ask the thousands of people we have helped across the globe.

When we adjust our thinking, and our nutrition, great things begin to happen. Remember, it is not God's will that we walk around in a state of sickness. Make these adjustments today.

108
Worth Something

DR. MICHELE

Lest we feel left out, I remind myself, and you, that Jesus considers us as worth something. We count with Him!

Therefore, I want to emphasize that Jesus died for what He counts as precious, the likes of you and me. That makes us "big" in His estimation of us. Which brings this scripture to mind.

"God proves His love for us in that while we were sinners, Christ died for us." (Romans 5:8)

We throw away "bad apples" and anything else that's begun to rot. However, in the "rotten" condition of our sinful hearts, Jesus died for us. He didn't die for nothing; He died for something valuable, someone like me and you.

We count with Jesus! In His eyes, we are not "nothings" without value, but "someones" with great value! Let's thank and praise God for making us worth something!

"He died for all, so that those who live might no longer live for themselves, but for Him who died and was raised for them" (2 Corinthians 5:15)

Someone made good ought to be good for something!

How about life's greatest purpose? Jesus wants us to live for Him, who made us good through His death and resurrection. He ever lives to share God's love with a "rotten," loveless world.

He continues to carry on this worthy love-mission by using us to be His mouth, hands, and feet to bring Good News. We are valuable and precious to God!

109
Never Give Up

DR. MICHELE

AFTER A WEEK OF CHALLENGES WITH FLIGHT DELAYS DUE TO WEATHER, it give one the chance to manage stress. Scripture comes to mind.

> *"We are hard pressed on every side, but not crushed; perplexed, but not in despair; persecuted, but not abandoned; struck down, but not destroyed. We always carry around in our body the death of Jesus, so that the life of Jesus may also be revealed in our body. For we who are alive are always being given over to death for Jesus' sake, so that His life may also be revealed in our mortal body."* (2 CORINTHIANS 4:8-11 NIV)

We are eternal beings. But this mortal skin-bag of flesh wants to react to the everyday stresses. That's when we call on our Savior through prayer and agreement! He will bring resurrection life to us.

Agreement is not only prayer while expecting results. Agreement is having our actions agree with God's Word. Action means we must be proactive in creating results! Negative action brings negative results, and positive action brings positive results. Results are not always instantaneous. Sometimes results come after years of hard labor and mental fortitude as the diamonds in the rough are polished.

Don't give up!

We are to be strong in his power and might! (Ephesians 6:10)

It's not always easy to find strength in challenge, especially if you are physically and mentally tired. Where do we turn? Of course, we go to the Word seeking direction. With good direction we can take right action.

In the meantime we continue to push through the storms of life and look on the bright side of all things, because we have so many gifts and blessings.

We remain truly blessed. We will also use right work and action to address the problems. Praise our Lord in advance, as help is on the way!

Today is a beautiful day. We have a strong at heart and mental attitude! We will survive the storms!

God is good, all the time.

110
Best Buddies

DR. MICHELE

WHAT IS A BUDDY? THE SCRIPTURE THAT PROMPTED THIS THOUGHT comes from Ecclesiastes 4:9-10 and reads:

> *"Two are better than one... If one falls down his friend ("Buddy") can help him up, but pity the man who falls and has no one to help him up."*

Seems that the Lord has created us to be connected with others, and not to be loners, doing life by ourselves.

From the beginning, we see this truth in the lives of Adam and Eve. Yes, and remember Noah? He, built the ark for his family's safety and the preservation of the human race along with the "two-by-twos" of other creatures.

When Jesus sent out His disciples to extend His ministry, the Gospel of Mark states that "He called the twelve and began to send them out two by two." (MARK 6:6)

After Pentecost, the 120 believers (men and women) along with those who had gathered in the upper room, did so because they needed the shared fellowship, encouragement, gifts, and strengths in their future mission together. Buddies!

Early in the life of the Church, and it still happens today, ministry very often happened in pairs. For example, Paul and Barnabas.(whose name means "encourager") traveled together throughout the Mediterranean area with the Gospel. Buddies indeed!

We still need buddies today, in our families, friendships, neighborhoods, jobs of all kinds, and in our church associations. Buddies provide what we individually don't have, or can't do.

I pray that we live as buddies to and for each other. Let's encourage someone today on the narrow road.

111
The First Secret to Resilience

DR. MARK

As we all are aware, our strength and resilience is always being tested. The silent enemy, some new flu variant, keeps popping up. Can it be stopped? How do we slow its spread? Can we protect ourselves? For now, let's address a different question: why is this virus so virulent?

There are two main definitive points of both causality and exacerbation. In this reading, let's discuss *fear*.

It is important to understand that our bodies are equipped with two main sources of protection. One being the nervous system, and the second being the immune system. It is the nervous system's job to monitor environmental signals, interpret them, and organize appropriate behavioral responses.

When the nervous system recognizes a threatening environmental stress, it alerts a vast community of cells to impending danger, and springs to action. As we know, there are certainly external threats to our system, such as in the extreme example of a lion chasing you for dinner. There are also internal threats, which are driven by our *interpretation* of our external surroundings. An example of this could be traumatic memories, replay of images, hearing threatening news, and repeating fearful proclamations.

Once our alarms are sounded, stress hormones are released into the blood which constrict blood vessels of the digestive tract, moving blood to preferentially nourish the tissues of the arms and legs to enable us to get out of harms way. Before the blood was sent to the extremities, it was concentrated in the visceral organs. Moving the blood from the viscera to the limbs in this fight or flight response results in the inhibition of other functions, namely the ability of our immune system to fight pathogenic bacteria or viruses.

Let's remember, when the immune system is mobilized, it takes up a lot of energy with the intent of fighting anything that is trying to attack us on the inside. So, once the fight or flight response is activated, the immune system is suppressed.

Here's the big problem. When the brain is confronted with two choices, to either activate the nervous system for a fight or flight response or to activate the immune system to fight these aforementioned bacterial or viral invaders, it always leans toward the fight or flight response. If you're on the couch nursing a cold and a lion crashes through the door, it makes sense that the priority would be to get up and fight, or run. Unlikely? Indeed. But consider how many opportunities to fear that today's world gives us, every hour of every day!

Endless news broadcasts, social media feeds, and stresses of work and family can sometimes bring fear. Add this to statements we might hear about our health:

"I hope I don't get the coronavirus."

"I'm afraid I'll get really sick."

"I am so scared of being around other people who might make me sick."

"Have you heard the pandemic is back?"

These statements are obviously fear-based. But, let's keep in mind, these statements do not need to be uttered out loud to create the same response. If we *think* fear, we will become fear. If our mind is filled with fearful ideas, we will become fear. If our eyes are continually reading statements of fear, we will, again, become fear. As you can see, these statements and actions will drive our fight or flight response and depress our immune system's ability to do what it was created to do, which is fight for us.

With this in mind, consider these questions:

Are you controlled by thoughts about faith or fear?

Do your conversations center around fear or faith?

Based on your lifestyle, and assuming there are no lions in your neighborhood, is there an underlying current of fear that's keeping your immune system from operating as the priority?

It is high time to understand that fear is the chosen language of our enemy. Let's not become experts in that language.

112
Rest Takes Practice

DR. MICHELE

Let's learn to appreciate and practice rest.

"Then He said to them all, 'If anyone desires to come after Me, let him deny himself, and take up his cross daily, and follow Me.'" (Luke 9:23)

Sometimes this passage can be misconstrued into a burden of working all the time. But even God rested on the seventh day of creation, and Jesus took a rest on the Sabbath day.

Sometimes saying that one extra "yes" to someone else means saying "no" to oneself and that ends up creating exhaustion, which impacts personal wellness. We may even end up in bitterness and despair. Rest does not mean being selfish. Rest is an act of self-kindness and self-love.

Rest fills up the tank. When we are well rested we have much more to give, and look forward to giving.

How are you practicing rest today?

113
Buckle Up

DR. MICHELE

Times can be confusing, as if there's a war between light and darkness. Seek peace in the Word of God and you will find it. The following scripture comes to mind:

> "Finally, be strong in the Lord and in his mighty power. Put on the full armor of God, so that you can take your stand against the devil's schemes.
>
> For our struggle is not against flesh and blood, but against the rulers, against the authorities, against the powers of this dark world and against the spiritual forces of evil in the heavenly realms.
>
> Therefore put on the full armor of God, so that when the day of evil comes, you may be able to stand your ground, and after you have done everything, to stand.
>
> Stand firm then, with the belt of truth buckled around your waist, with the breastplate of righteousness in place, and with your feet fitted with the readiness that comes from the gospel of peace.
>
> In addition to all this, take up the shield of faith, with which you can extinguish all the flaming arrows of the evil one.
>
> Take the helmet of salvation and the sword of the Spirit, which is the word of God." (Ephesians 6)

Buckle up with the full armor of God. In times of uncertainty, using the shield of faith will thwart all the darts of darkness. No enemy formed against us shall prosper!

Fear not friends, our almighty Father knows the beginning from the end, and every step in between.

Let's put on the full armor of God. Stay the course. Never let disappointment pull you off course! God has your back, your front, your sides, your top, and your bottom!

114
Our Advocate

DR. MICHELE

I stumbled onto this passage while looking for some inspiration.

> "If anyone does sin, we have an advocate with the Father, Jesus Christ the righteous, and He is the atoning sacrifice for our sins, and not for ours only, but for the sins of the whole world." (I JOHN 2:1-2)

Think about this for a moment. Heaven provides a lawyer (advocate) for law breakers (those who break God's laws) on planet earth! He has a world of clients and serves everyone without cost. When Jesus pleads a case before the courtroom of heaven, He never loses. Everyone who asks for Him to advocate for them is successful in finding mercy.

Good lawyers instill hope in tenuous situations. Good lawyers know the law, and how to apply it in ways that will set their clients free of all charges against them. Jesus knows well the laws of the Kingdom of God and how they apply on earth. In fact, His life on earth bears witness that He never sinned as scripture makes clear:

> "He was tempted in all points as we are, yet without sin."
> (HEBREWS 4:15)

Jesus knew the law and, when tempted, He didn't break it. More than that, He took our place on the cross (the place of God's judgement) as the sinless sacrifice for the sins of all. This advocate, unlike earthly lawyers, paid all the fees of God's Kingdom, through His death on the cross.

The amazing good news is this: He satisfied the law of God in our place! Now, we are set free of all charges and escape the judgment of condemnation! And, there's more. Jesus keeps on advocating on our behalf.

Now we know that whenever we break God's laws, or are being persecuted, we can call on Him to advocate for us. He wins every time!! What a hope-giver our Savior is!

115
Set Your Sights

DR. MICHELE

Once in a while, I hear something like, "Set your sights high" or, "What kind of a mindset is that?"

This Scripture comes to my mind:

> "If you have been raised with Christ, seek the things that are above. Set your minds on things that are above, not on things that are on earth." (Colossians 3:1-2)

Mindsets refer to determined life patterns. We choose to think or act in ways developed over the years on the basis of what we've learned. Perhaps, even somewhat unintentionally, we've picked what seems to work for us. So now let us reconsider.

Do I really think high enough so as to establish the best mindset and life patterns?

The above verses challenge us to re-think or test ourselves on these issues. I get the idea that I need to distinguish between *my* priorities and what really counts most. Another verse pops up.

> "All that is in the world, the desires of the flesh, the desire of the eyes, the pride of riches, comes not from the Father, but from the world. The world and its desire are passing away, but those who do the will of the Father live forever." (I John 2:16-17)

Mankind seems to have a propensity for clinging to an "earthy" mindset and setting our sights too low. We need constant reminders that the world and what it offers will eventually pass away, while what comes from God lasts eternally.

Through the Holy Spirit, our loving God will correct our mindsets and help set our sights high, where we "see," think about, and hear Him!

God so wanted to give us life that He went to love's extreme by offering His only Son (our Lord and Savior, Jesus Christ) to die for that to happen. Since God set His sights on setting us free, let's set our sights on being all we can be, in Him today!

116
Your Real Ministry Begins

DR. MICHELE

When the day, or week, comes to an end, do you find yourself exhausted from the challenges? Do you want to close yourself in a dark room and retreat? Do you notice yourself giving your family and key relationships your mere "leftovers"?

In Malachi 1, God rebukes his people for bringing lame and blind animals to sacrifice. They were giving what had little value (their leftovers).

I remember as a new wife and business leader when I would walk through the door into my home, the Lord would say to me, "Now your real ministry begins."

God was saying my home assignment was more important than my work assignment. As a physician I often give late into the day, and most weekends, to meet the needs of hurting people. I realized then, as I still do, that if my family and those closest to me do not respect me as being genuine, authentic, and able to meet their needs, then I needed to make some big adjustments in my life and priorities.

I began asking some soul-searching questions?

Was I leaving no reserve for my home and those closest to me?

Was I emotionally drained and unavailable at home?

Had I given everything I had at the office? Was there anything left?

For those of us who give it all and leave little left for our loved ones, we need to re evaluate our priorities. Perhaps we need to truly leave our weekends for family, rest, and prayer. We have to find our personal rhythm. The sabbath was set in motion for a reason!

Mark and I do not want to look back and realize that we have given our home and family our leftovers. All things in balance can be a challenge, but living with right priorities is worth it!

What changes might you need to make to enjoy the narrow road with God, family, and friends?

117
Abiding Protection

DR. MICHELE

The "normal" Christian life is a humble, dependent, successful live (be careful how you define "success") lived in relationship with Jesus.

Here are a few examples of *normal* for Christians.

We are "yoked" to Jesus, our Savior and Redeemer (Matthew 11:30) going the same direction, traveling the same speed, and arriving at the same destination at the same time as Him.

We "abide" with Him (John 15), find our nurture in Him, are attached to Him at all times, and are subject to correction and pruning for our own good; we are diligent to not only enter His rest (Hebrews 4:11) but also to stay in the throne room of God in confident expectancy that He has only good for us.

The key here is our continuing relationship with Jesus, our source of life and hope. It is this posture and dynamic by which we "qualify" for the protections spoken of in Psalm 91.

I wonder if the seeming disconnect between our experience and the promises of Psalm 91 is of our own making. When we enter into relationship with God through Christ (salvation), all the promises of God are "yes and amen." But, if on our part we do not continue in the relationship with Jesus as Lord but wander from Him in day-to-day living, do we not also separate ourselves from His day-to-day "secret place" protection?

We can never separate ourselves from His love (Romans 8), but we can certainly make the mistake of not walking in it.

Think of having an umbrella but not using it on a rainy day. Think of having a ready, willing, and able Friend but not depending on Him. Think of not accessing a bountiful bank account under the guise of independent "self-sufficiency." Bad idea.

"Be sober, on alert" as we are encouraged in 1Peter 5:8,9, because "Your enemy the devil prowls around like a roaring lion looking for someone to devour." The sober, alert place is in the abiding, resting holy place described in Psalm 91. It is there we find protection from every harm; there is where we experience these promises.

> *"He who dwells in the shelter of the Most High will abide in the shadow of the Almighty.*
>
> *I will say to the LORD, "You are my refuge and my fortress, my God, in whom I trust."*
>
> *Surely, He will deliver you from the snare of the fowler, and from the deadly plague.*
>
> *He will cover you with His feathers; under His wings you will find refuge; His faithfulness is a shield and rampart.*
>
> *You will not fear the terror of the night, nor the arrow that flies by day, nor the pestilence that stalks in the darkness, nor the calamity that destroys at noon.*
>
> *Though a thousand may fall at your side, and ten thousand at your right hand, no harm will come near you.*
>
> *You will only see it with your eyes and witness the punishment of the wicked.*
>
> *Because you have made the LORD your dwelling—my refuge, the Most High— no evil will befall you, no plague will approach your tent.*
>
> *For He will command His angels concerning you to guard you in all your ways.*

They will lift you up in their hands, so that you will not strike your foot against a stone.

You will tread on the lion and cobra; you will trample the young lion and serpent.

"Because he loves Me, I will deliver him; because he knows My name, I will protect him.

When he calls out to Me, I will answer him; I will be with him in trouble. I will deliver him and honor him.

With long life I will satisfy him and show him My salvation."

    We know that prayer is our connection with God. Think of it this way, when you keep the lines of communication open, you are doing your part to abide. When you rest in Him, you are trusting Him for Your care.
    When you draw near to God, He will draw near to you.

_____

_____

_____

_____

_____

_____

_____

118
Let There Be Light

DR. MICHELE

Recently, Mark and I attended a music concert that used these words from Isaiah 60:1-3:

"Arise, shine, for your Light has come and the glory of the Lord rises upon you! See, darkness covers the earth..., but the Lord rises upon you and His glory appears over you. nations will come to your light..."

Talk about a bright light! How many lumens would that be? Surely, we can't even imagine the spectacle.

In His teachings, Jesus makes it clear that He is the light of the world (John 8:12) and that His followers would be also. (Matt. 5:14)

Me, and you, a light? Yes!

So we sing: "This little light of mine, I'm gonna let it shine."

Darkness is a part of our physical world, but also part of the spiritual world. There's also mental and moral darkness. For every type of darkness, Jesus is the light! We can live in the light *and* be lights in the darkness of our world.

Jesus shines through us to "turn on the light" for others living in the darkness of evil.

What a joy for us to not only walk in the "Jesus" light, but also enable others to do so also. Praise the Lord for this honor and privilege!

How can you shine with Jesus' light today?

_____

_____

_____

119
Mysterious Ways

DR. MICHELE

The famous Italian poet of the Middle Ages, Dante, penned these words: "The Lord works in mysterious ways His wonders to perform." Such words stimulated my thoughts today on Psalm 145:3-5.

"Great is the Lord and greatly to be praised; His greatness is unsearchable. One generation shall laud Your works to another, and shall declare Your mighty acts."

We often get caught up in thinking the great "works" are ours, yet they are His, given to us to develop and flourish. The ego wants to receive praise, but as we walk the narrow road with God, we desire to give all praise to Him.

Dante, being a devout Catholic Christian, often utilized scriptural thoughts in his many dramatic and poetic works. Deeply pondering God's "wondrous works" and Holy Word, opens our eyes to more and more of His "mysterious ways."

Thank God, the Holy Spirit constantly works with us enabling us to grow in how our loving heavenly Father wants us to live, if we are sensitive and listening.

We are his children! In Him we live and move and have our being! Every day may His light, shine through us for all to see!

120
The Enemy of Progress

DR. MICHELE

This past week ministering to people in my practice shed light on how harboring envy can destroy the spirit and keep it from growth.

"The spirit of envy can destroy; it can never build." (Margaret Thatcher, former British Prime Minister).

Envy is the enemy of progress. Why be envious of someone else when God supplies all of our needs? Why do we forget our Gods promises?

"My God shall supply all my needs according to His riches in glory." (Philippians 4:19)

What a waste to dwell in envy of another person! Let go and trust God. He keeps his promises.

Remember to give God the glory for the needs he provides. "Blessed be the Lord, who daily loads me with benefits." (Psalm 68:19)

When we are envious we likely have a hurt at the root of our being. There is an unhealed wound or a sense of lack.

"Hurting people, hurt people" the expression goes. That's how pain patterns get passed on, generation after generation after generation. Break the chain today.

"Meet anger with sympathy, contempt with compassion, cruelty with kindness, and envy with love. Greet grimaces with smiles, forgive and forget about finding fault. Love is the weapon of the future." (Mother Teresa)

Let's be grateful for our blessings today, and thankful for God's riches and glory. What are you thankful for today?

121
Promises in the Wilderness

DR. MICHELE

When it seems like we are in the wilderness we know God is ever-present and with us. This is when refinement happens and we have the opportunity to go deeper in our spiritual journey.

Scripture reminds us to be lighthearted for the Lord is our Shepard. (Psalms 23) He is also our inspiration.

> *"Now may God, the inspiration and fountain of hope, fill you to overflowing with uncontainable joy and perfect peace as you trust in Him. And may the power of the Holy Spirit continually surround your life with His superabundance until you radiate with hope!"* (Romans 15:13 tpt)

Pause and think on those edifying words. Inspiration, joy, peace, superabundance, and hope!

In rocky times, pray. Pray without ceasing. Pray relentlessly on your knees. Rest assured that our Lord hears and will restore the spirit of hope and inspiration.

Look up, look around, breathe in a fresh new breath and renew your mind. This is a new day!

Pray the following with intention:

> *Lord, help me never forget the promises You've made to me, for they are my hope and confidence.* (Psalm 119:49)

What promises are you holding on to today?

122
The Best Decision

DR. MICHELE

I love the word *love*. Love requires a decision. Think for a moment about the difference between living by feelings versus living by decisions.

All of us have times of not wanting to do important things (including important commitments), but successful people find a way to do what is right, regardless of emotions.

There are times in relationships where we "feel" love, but there are also times when we don't. One of the most important revelations we can receive is understanding love is not just a feeling, it is a decision.

Jesus is truly our example in this. "Greater love has no one than this, than to lay down one's life for his friends." (John 15:13). It can be a challenge to live with love when people have wounded your soul, darkened your heart and created skepticism. But His Word is clear.

"Thou shalt love thy neighbor as thyself." (Mark 12:31)

Living from feelings and wounds can twist this into "Do unto others as they have done unto you." Oops! Wrong answer. This approach will continue the viscous cycle of bitterness instead of the healing decision to love!

Revenge is toxic and only further destroys a person's well being and relationships. Live love, not simply to be a good person. Living love allows for healing and growth.

"Love is patient, love is kind. It does not envy, it does not boast, it is not proud.

It does not dishonor others, it is not self-seeking, it is not easily angered, it keeps no record of wrongs.
Love does not delight in evil but rejoices with the truth.
It always protects, always trusts, always hopes, always perseveres.
Love never fails." (1 Corinthians 13:4-8)

Free yourself to live by making the decision to love.
Who do you need to decide to love today?

123

Resisting Distancing

DR. MICHELE

I SEE SO MUCH PAIN IN PEOPLES LIVES, AND HURTS THAT ARE CARRIED forward, that need to be put to rest so that we can grow, give the love needed, and receive love in return.

Regularly withdrawing our heart from those who disappoint us yields pain.

"Love is patient, love is kind." (1 Corinthians 13:4) People of all ages frequently allow themselves to become distant and detached from people who do not meet their expectations or who hurt their hearts. Then we live in that withdrawal mode.

"Husbands, love your wives as Christ loved the church." (EPHESIANS 5:25) The marriage relationship is an example of how we can live in all relationships. This does not mean we won't have boundaries in our relationships, but it does mean we are to lean into heart connections and not away from them. (And it certainly does not mean we have to tolerate abuse!)

Instead of becoming distant with a hardened heart, dig into the root of the hurt and pain, and find resolution! There is no need to harden your heart because one person (or a handful of people) wounded you. The world will fail us. People will fail us. We will fail ourselves. But God will never fail us!

Growing through pain allows blossoming and fruit. Staying in pain equals bitterness and disdain. That is really where the pain is. We let the past eat us and eat our ability to experience abundant life.

Look into your roots of hurt and pain. Maybe it is time, with God's help, to let go and love!

124
We Learn to Choose

DR. MICHELE

"Anyone who does not love does not know God, because God is love." (1John 4:8)

Love fiercely, forgive often, and play hard.

As the saying goes, *in the blink of an eye, everything can change!* Many of us have been faced with life tragedies where, in an instant, things change. And in many cases they don't just change for an instant, they change forever. This can mean broken lives, broken families, broken finances, and broken hearts.

We can either live broken or do something with the situation and rise up!

"We have troubles all around us, but we are not defeated! We do not know what to do, but we do not give up hope of living! We are persecuted, but God does not leave us. We are hurt sometimes, but we are not destroyed." (2 Corinthians 4:8-9)

When affliction comes, it is easy to hate, get angry, and be troubled. This emotion and disease of brokenness (yes it is a *dis*-ease) does no good. Instead it robs us from true joy and the true abundance of life.

So what do we do about all this pain, this sense of dis-ease? We learn to choose love, and to love passionately and deeply!

"This is my command: Love each other as I have loved you. The greatest love a person can show is to die for his friends. You are my friends if

you do what I command you... This is my command: Love each other."
(JOHN 15:12-14,17)

May we love one another as Christ loved us, and showed his love for us!

Love, no matter the circumstance. In the center of love there is no dis-ease or fear; there is peace.

DRS. MARK & MICHELE
SHERWOOD

Mark Sherwood, Naturopathic Doctor (ND) and Michele L. Neil-Sherwood, Doctor of Osteopathy (DO), have a full-time wellness-based medical practice called the Functional Medical Institute where they adopt a whole person approach, which is outcome-based for each individual's unique needs.

Their goal is to lead people down a pathway of true healing. To that end, there are two purposes:

1. To eradicate all self-imposed, choice driven disease conditions.
2. To eliminate the usage of unnecessary medications. Through their unique clinic, various diagnostic tests are used, healing and prevention of common disease patterns are the norm.

The couple has co-authored three bestselling books. They have been seen on national TV, been quoted on CNN, featured on ABC, CBS, NBC, FOX and CBN, and are regular contributors to many national publications.

Drs. Mark and Michele appear on many TV networks with their show, *Furthermore*. They are also movie actors and producers with several films and millions of views.

Their influence also expands into healthy meal and product development with the formulations of Kingdom Fuel, Kingdom Kandy, Kingdom Kup, and other proprietary foods.

The couple understands the importance of nutrition, medical food & supplementation, exercise prescription, rest, stress management, hormone balance, and DNA analysis. This makes them a modern day "dynamic duo of wellness."

Dr. Michele is a former national physique champion, taekwondo black belt, and judo black belt. As a fitness and functional medicine expert, she is a fellow in Osteopathic Internal Medicine and an IFM certified practitioner. Along with Dr. Mark, she instructs clinicians worldwide on nutrigenomics and nutrigenetics.

Dr. Mark has completed training and certifications in age management, nutrigenetics, nutrigenomics, peptide therapy, hormone therapy, stress management, GI health, and immunology.

He is a 24-year retired veteran of the Tulsa Police Department, where he logged a decade of service on the department's SWAT Team. He is also a former Oklahoma state and regional bodybuilding champion, and ex-professional baseball player. Dr. Mark was a 2022 gubernatorial candidate for Oklahoma. Additionally, Dr. Mark traveled the world for over ten years with the world-famous Power Team.

For free resources and updates, please visit www.Sherwood.TV.

INVITE DRS. MICHELE AND MARK TO SPEAK AT YOUR EVENT!

With their extensive backgrounds in naturopathic medicine and personal development, they offer a comprehensive approach to physical, mental, and spiritual well-being.

Together, they have built a reputation for their dynamic speaking engagements, where they educate and inspire audiences with their combined expertise, empowering individuals to take control of their health and live their best lives.

FEATURED IN

TBN · NBC · CBS · abc · CNN · THE HUFFINGTON POST
FOX NEWS · FamilyCircle · First · CBN NEWS · SHAPE · U.S. News

Surviving the Garden of Eatin'

Surprising Biblical Insights to Enjoy Optimal Wellness

sherwood.tv/books

Fork Your Diet

Master the Four Fundamentals of Good Health

sherwood.tv/books

The Quest for Wellness

A Practical and Personal Wellness Plan for Optimal Health

sherwood.tv/books

OUR MOVIES

The Sherwoods have produced several acclaimed, wholesome films with more in production.

Learn more, and stream here: https://sherwood.tv/videos/

Dr. Michele and Dr. Mark have developed a proprietary line of Kingdom products for your health and enjoyment.

Kingdom Fuel: Meal replacement shake mix

Kingdom Kandy: Delicious protein bars
Kingdom Kup: Organic, mold-free coffee
Please visit shop.fmidr.com and enjoy 10% off with code "First10"

KINGDOM FUEL
Your Simple Start to a Transformed Life

If you're looking for positive change in your health, can I recommend Kingdom fuel? Developed by my friends, Drs. Michele and Mark Sherwood, A complete meal replacement, or a boost for your workouts. I enjoy it, and hope you'll give it a try.
—Kevin Sorbo, actor and filmmaker

FUNCTIONAL MEDICAL INSTITUTE

WE CARE FOR THE WHOLE PERSON
No matter where you live, the Functional Medical Institute Staff can serve you, in-person or via tele-health.

CARE FOR THE WHOLE PERSON
Make lasting changes to live a longer, healthier life.

SCIENCE-BASED APPROACH TO HEALTH
Lifestyle Adjustments that Last

UNIQUE AND PERSONAL PLANS
Diagnostics, Experience, and Proven Results

WWW.FMIDR.COM

WWW.SHERWOOD.TV

Made in the USA
Monee, IL
08 November 2023